Published by Harwell/Lewis Publishing Company
P.O. Box 3385, Lakeland, Florida 33802.

ISBN No. 0-9764436-2-7

For sales information call (863) 688-2665.

Around the House

Simple Stories of Heart and Home

Wilson Adams

Dedication

To Julie

Thank you for sharing your smile
and bringing light to my life.

Acknowledgements

Thanking people is a risky venture, as there exists the ever-present danger of leaving out someone. I must try.

To Brent Lewis, who first suggested that my stuff was worth publishing, I owe a debt of gratitude. Brent is a consummate professional and without him, there would be no book. He painstakingly edited the stories, added the pictures, and put this thing together. Thank you, my friend.

Drew and Mandy Christenson, editors of the local newspaper, the Browser Connection, were kind enough to run my stories each week. A special thanks to them and all the gang at the Connection.

To my neighbors and friends in White House, Tennessee who read my column each week and who stopped me in the store or at the ballpark to tell me that a story had brought a smile to their day, thank you. A special word of appreciation goes to my Kentucky friend, David Lanphear, who encourages me with friendship beyond words. Together we have shared laughter and tears. And to Shaun Adams who took the picture on the back of this book. It's hard to make some people look good.

And to my parents... Mom has gone to live in a better place, but her sense of humor lives on in her son. She loved to laugh. Dad always had a gift for writing and a penchant for perfection–even to the point of correcting my spelling in personal letters. It helped. And to four wonderful children who have had to endure public stories about their private lives–a special thank you to Sharon, Dale, Crystal, and Luke. Your father loves you more than you can imagine.

And to Julie Anne... Thank you for encouraging me to write. My heart smiles because of you.

The Front Porch

A lot has changed in America the last few years but perhaps no change has had a more dramatic impact on family life than the disappearance of the front porch. More issues were resolved on America's front porches than in any other place, yet so few are being used today. They have become antiquated relics of times past as modern families have moved behind fences, to back decks, or merely indoors.

My wife says every home needs two things: a fireplace and a front porch. I think she's right. I have a theory behind the popularity of the Cracker Barrel restaurant chain. It's not just the country cooking that keeps America coming back for more. It's those Tennessee rocking chairs and the cozy front porch atmosphere. Thirty minute wait? No problem. Let's go rock a spell.

It's amazing how a few minutes of quiet reflection on the front porch can calm a frazzled mind after a hectic day. It's also the best place for personal and family therapy. I've noticed talks with teenagers go better on the front porch than anywhere else. Give us a cup of coffee and enough "porch time" and my wife and I can solve just about any national or local problem. Come to think of it, international summit meetings between world leaders would probably accomplish a lot more if they were held on a front porch.

I watched the sun set from our front porch a few nights ago. I waved at a few passing cars that drove down our country lane. I heard the distinct puttering sound of an approaching tractor and watched as it rolled past. And I saw the moon begin to rise. It was God's exclamation point to a wonderful day.

I was raised without PlayStations, videos, and CDs. Not knowing we were deprived of such things, we simply used our imagination, invented our own games, and played in the yard until darkness took over. Then we would cool off on the front porch, sip a "Co-Cola" (as my grandmother would say), and listen in as the older folks talked and told humorous tales of times past.

I hope when my kids are grown and gone and begin to choose houses of their own, that they keep in mind the need for a good front porch. After all, their father may wish to visit now and then and when he does, he'll need a good place to end the day.

A Mother's Day Cookbook

I get busy sometimes. Too busy. But God has a unique way of slowing me down and reminding me of what is important—He gave me four children. Sometimes I think God gives us children to raise and we end up learning more *from* them than we give *to* them.

My kids have taught me a lot of things. They have taught me to slow down and live the moments. They have taught me that everything I think is important, isn't. They have taught me patience, and love, and most of all, the joy of simple things.

A couple years ago, our youngest brought home a *Mother's Day Cookbook*—the ingenious idea of a creative teacher named Buffey Briley who teaches at his elementary school. If ever there was a school project labeled a "keeper," this is it.

May I share with you the simple thoughts of some of the kids when it comes to cooking?

A little girl named Brooke gave her recipe for Chicken Nachos. ***Ingredients***: "5 corn chips, 2 gallons of white cheese, 1 can brown beans, 1 jar of taco sauce, and 1 little container of sour cream." (Chicken nachos for cheese lovers, I guess).

Brandon gave us his recipe for pizza which included: ***Ingredients***: "5 pepperoni, 6 teaspoons of cheese, 7 pieces of bread, 8 gallons of red sauce, and 10 pounds of juicy ham." (I like a pizza-maker who doesn't skimp on the extras!!) He also added that you should "cook the pizza in the microwave for 100 minutes until it looks like pizza." Smart thinking.

A little boy named Tucker has it down when it comes to chocolate pie: ***Ingredients***: "1 crust, 2 plain chocolates, 1 pack of calf-slobber." (Chocolate pie that only a mother would love.)

Finally, our little guy included his world-famous recipe for a peanut butter and jelly sandwich. ***Ingredients***: "2 halves of bread, 2 jars of jelly, 2 jars of peanut butter." (Nothing cheap about *his* PBJ's).

Refreshingly simple. It is impossible to read this wonderful little cookbook and frown. And while it will never attain the status of a Betty Crocker "how to" in the kitchen, I will tell you this: it's number one around our house!

Thank you, Mrs. Briley, and all other teachers for sharing your days with our children and for filling up our refrigerator doors and memory boxes with priceless treasures from their childhood. Years from now when he has left for college and we are alone, two weepy parents will go slowly through the treasures of yesteryear and relive these precious days. Then ... we'll probably get up and go to the kitchen and make us one of those world-famous peanut-butter and jelly sandwiches.

A Letter from Home

Dear Son:

In the aftermath of the terror attack on 9-11 and in preview of coming war, I am writing to say three very special words: I love you. The events of the past few days have caused parents all across the country to stop and re-think their priorities about their loved ones. If any good can come out of such a horrible and senseless tragedy, maybe this is something.

Son, neither my generation nor yours knows the horrors of war. I was born a few years after the end of World War II and too young to know about the Korean War. I do remember growing up with the gruesome pictures of Vietnam. I missed going to Southeast Asia by one decade although I knew people who went there—and died there.

You and your college classmates can recall Desert Storm and the Persian Gulf War but that conflict was rather one-sided and over quickly.

There is no way to know where this war will take us because it will be a different kind of war. Islamic nations may say they stand with us against terrorism but when religious pressure mounts, anything can happen. All of which means, it is imperative that we trust in God. Look closely at the backside of a dollar bill. If there was ever a time to start trusting, it is *now.*

I'm thankful that we have a president who isn't afraid to admit his faith or to ask his nation to pray. And son, when you pray, remember to pray for him and for the leaders around him. It's one of the greatest things you can do for your country.

And fly the flag. That flag is stained with the blood, sweat, and tears of generations past who have sacrificed and died in order that we might be free. Fly it proudly, son. And when you go to a ballgame and hear the words of Francis Scott Key, stand at attention, put your hand over your heart and sing the song. Nothing gripes me more than seeing young people milling about and talking during the national anthem. That song is about a flag that stands for freedom—a freedom that hasn't come cheap. And they need to know something else: no one is going to take that away. No one.

I know there are racial, religious, and geographical differences in this country, but not today. Like a family that often bickers but is quick to rally around their wounded, so America stands as one. For good or bad, we may pick on each other but no one comes into our backyard and picks on us. Those who make that mistake will be in for a fight they could not imagine. And they will lose.

One more thing... if I could see you today, I would hug you a little longer and a little tighter.

I love you, Dad.

Rampant Inactivity

I am a fan of the political process. Even though there are two subjects supposedly off limits in public circles of conversation—politics and religion—I find myself at times crossing the line on both. Somehow each of the forbidden topics seems to be more interesting fodder for casual gab than ... say, the weather. (Although dialoguing with a stranger about the weather is probably safer turf upon which to stand.)

During the political season of 2004, I saw a mini-van bearing the sticker: "Bush-Cheney." I spotted the owner and feigned shock and awe that someone had played such an awful prank of political proportions on their mode of transportation. Later, I saw another vehicle bearing the bumper advertisement of "Kerry-Edwards." I pulled up to the light and was about to follow through with the same comic routine but the guy driving the Kerry car looked a lot bigger than I was. "Nice weather," I said.

Politics. Is there a crazier world than the one of political spin-and-grin? Everyone knows that politicians schmooze older people, kiss babies, and promise everything. And why not? That's what politicians do. And we fall for it. "We're going to reduce the deficit while having all of these really neat government programs to feed, clothe, and house everyone." Jobs? "No problem." Health-care? "No problem." Threats from terrorists? "No problem–fact is, if I'm elected everyone will like us–including the French."

Do we really think that the next occupant of 1600 Pennsylvania Avenue will solve everything and make all the bad go away? Okay, maybe I'm a tad bit cynical but I don't think so.

When I lived in suburban Maryland, I used to enjoy taking visitors to the Capitol building in Washington, D.C. and sit in the House Chambers watching our elected leaders give spirited speeches about some program of interest to the folks back home. The only problem was that the chambers would be completely empty save for the TV cameras and a few tourists in the gallery. But I suppose that it played well on the evening news back in Des Moines or Peoria. *Gotcha!*

You have to love the political conventions. This particular election year the Democrats are spinning in Bean-town while the Republicans are swinging away in the Big Apple. Beans and apples–I think that's what it comes down to.

Which brings me to my favorite political commentator of all time: David Brinkley. Brinkley covered twenty-two political conventions in his storied career of broadcast journalism and I loved to spend every fourth year listening to his dry wit. My favorite "Brinkley-ism" occurred at a Republican gathering a few years back when things seemed to be at a standstill. Brinkley made the following observation without cracking a smile, "There seems to be a lot of rampant inactivity occurring at the podium..." *Rampant inactivity*–an oxymoron any place other than a political convention.

Politics. It's crazy. And fun.

Church Scam Artists

Every church in town has them—people who stop by religious services with a tale of woe looking for a handout. You know the routine. The man sends in the woman while he waits out in the car (more sympathy that way) and she asks for money. Usually they are traveling and have car trouble or need gas and food. And usually... they just want C•A•S•H.

I stopped giving cash a long time ago—experience has taught me better. A friend, however, was tempted to give cash the other day when he read the sign held high by an unkempt fellow. It said: "I WILL NOT LIE—NEED MONEY FOR BEER." At least he was honest.

Last week I spoke to a church in Bowling Green, Kentucky. A fellow entered the service pushing a woman in a wheelchair. He dropped her off and went out to sit in the truck (I told you—the guy always waits outside). The church people spoke to them separately and found their stories to be conflicting—something about trying to get to

Michigan to the bedside of a dying relative and needing money for a broken water pump.

On Sunday night of the same week, this *same couple* showed up at our place of worship. Same M.O. – he pushes her in and waits in the truck. A different twist this time—now they were on the way to the bedside of a dying relative in Jackson, Mississippi (these people sure have a lot of dying relatives). A kind officer with the local police department stopped by and gave the Kentucky couple some simple advice: find the interstate and head north.

All of this reminds me of a man in southern California who became known for showing up at church services, coming forward at the end, and wanting to be baptized. Of course, as soon as the baptism was over and before he was even dry, he conned the naïve congregation out of money. Weeks later, Floyd Thompson of Garden Grove, California was speaking to a New Mexico church when in walked this same fellow. Same deal—end of service, he wanted to be baptized and join the good church.

This time, brother Thompson took to the floor and with the penitent looking fellow sitting on the front row, exposed the con man. "This man," Thompson stated, "wants to be baptized. I don't know why—because I baptized him a few months ago myself. He has gone to churches all over the southwest—and as soon as he is baptized, he is going to ask you for money..." Before my brother could finish, the fellow jumped from his front row seat and *ran* up the aisle and out the door. *Gotcha!*

Some things are funnier than fiction!

Congratulating the Graduates

In the spring of 2000, I spoke at a college commencement exercise in Florida. I was supposed to say something profound and brilliant. What I said was...

"It seems to me that after four years of majoring in e-mail, sending out for pizza, and hitting the snooze bar, my main job today is to make parents feel like they have done a good thing by investing much of their hard earned money in securing for you the finest in a college education. But here's the sad truth: *We're broke!* Because of your college tuition, we parents are at the chapter you never read in the library—*Chapter 11*!

"And to those who figure a college degree earns you the right to move back home with us—*wake up and smell the rent*!

"The truth is... because college cost so much, your mom and dad have had to move—to Motel 6. And contrary to what you've heard, we will not be leaving the light on for you.

"To those of you who have parents fortunate enough to ward off mortgage foreclosure, there's good news and bad news. The *good news* is: your parents still have the same address you had when you left for school. The *bad news* is: we have redecorated your room. It is now the guest room. Webster defines guest as a 'temporary visitor.'

"So today you turn from the ivory tower of education to the real world of aluminum siding, ready to hit the ground running (by the way, that is a 'mixed metaphor'—something you would have known if you hadn't cut English class in October!). I have a simple question: How is it that we spend thousands of dollars sending you to college and you still send us e-mail without punctuation and all in lower case? I don't get it.

"On such an august occasion as this I should probably quote the great philosopher Aristotle or Plato. Come to think of it, wasn't it one of those guys who said, 'When in doubt: *Get a job*!'

College. Some things never change. Congratulations!

Homecoming

Of all the holidays listed on the calendar, *Thanksgiving* gets my vote. It is the one holiday that exists without the crass (defined by Webster as "money-grubbing") commercialism of retailers seeking to capitalize on the spending habits of consumers. Well, sort of. The quiet and reflective family gathering of the fourth Thursday in November is followed by the free-for-all-Friday that officially opens the Christmas spending season. So much for nostalgic tranquility.

But for one day of the year we came home to family and friends. And we should.

Thanksgiving... The day means different things to different people, but to me it will always be synonymous with one word: *homecoming*. It is a holiday that is best epitomized by what awaits at the end of the road: roast turkey and mashed potatoes, giblet gravy and pumpkin pie for sure, but it is so much more.

Thanksgiving...provides for more than hearty appetites; it is a day that provides for a family's soul—a hearty homecoming for loved ones seldom seen. It's a special gathering of brothers and sisters who are separated by years as well as miles, of nieces and nephews, aunts and uncles, grandkids and grandparents. It's a day to be savored; to be lingered upon; to be reminded of where we've been while being thankful for the familial roots that call us home again.

Thanksgiving...It's a day to pause and reflect upon the simple. You know, the stuff that really matters. It's moms and grandmoms poring over family albums and reminiscing of days past. It's touch football in the side yard and heart to heart talks in the back bedroom. It's kids home from college and married kids on the phone wishing they could somehow be in two places at one time.

Thanksgiving...It's the snores of grown men drowning out a ballgame that blares in the background. It's a meal that took two days to prepare and twenty minutes to devour. It's a fire in the hearth and a mess in the kitchen. It's the same Uncle Martin who said, "I'm so full I won't eat again for a week!"—who starts grazing at sunset in search of leftovers. And it's the same old family stories year after year that cause us to smile and laugh year after year.

Thanksgiving...The journey gets complicated and the road takes us far away but each year there is one special day that calls us back to a place that will forever remain in our hearts. Yes, in a world of uncertainty and change, one thing remains the same: the joy of a warm and hearty *Welcome Home!*

It's called...*Thanksgiving.*

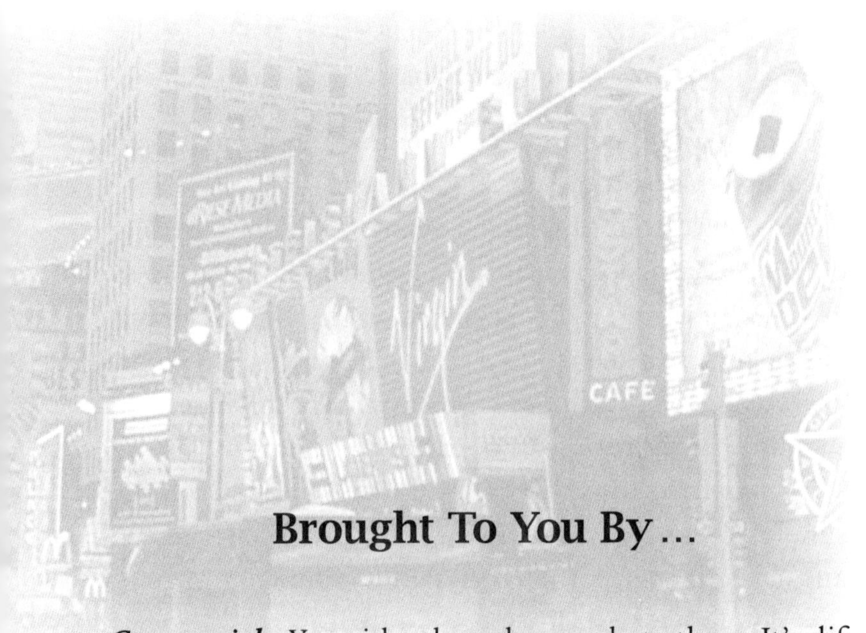

Brought To You By...

Commercials. You either love them or hate them. It's difficult to watch a thirty-minute sit-com and maintain any semblance of continuity because of the commercials. For example, a thirty-minute program is reduced to a *seventeen-minute* production because of the constant advertising interruptions. Which brings up "the" question—(no, not the age-old stumper, "What came first, the chicken or the egg?"—which as one little boy said, "What difference does it make—'cause we eat both of 'em!")—but the bigger inquiry: are we more entertained by the shows or by the commercials that sponsor them?

I vote for the latter.

How many baby-boomers fail to recall some of the earlier jingles by the Coca-Cola Company? *"I'd like to teach the world to sing in perfect harmony..."* Remember that one? It ranks up there with that infamous Disney ride—*"It's A Small World After All..."*—you know, the one you can't get out of your head for a week! Or the McDonald's ad that appealed to our selfish instincts —*"You deserve a break today..."* We bought into that one—so did our cholesterol!

And everyone knows that the beer commercials are the best—at least from an advertising perspective. I mean, who isn't captured by the holiday spirit as the Anheuser-Busch Clydesdales pull the jingle-bell sleigh through the snowy Vermont countryside? But come on. Maybe we should see the sleigh driver, with a little too much Budweiser on his breath, involved in a head-on collision with Santa Claus and his bunch. Wouldn't that be a touch more realistic?

Remember those old "Joe Isuzu" ads from the 80's? America fell in love with them because they were so off-the-wall dishonest. Everything that "Joe Isuzu" said about the Isuzu automobile was an obvious lie—"An Isuzu only costs $9, gets 94 m.p.g. and if you buy one this week, we'll throw in a *free* house!" Superimposed on the screen were the words: "He's lying!" Interestingly, Isuzu sales rose 21% during that ad campaign. (Which probably says more about us than about them.)

Perhaps the kicker came this morning when I was at the bedside of a friend getting ready to have serious surgery. We talked, and prayed, and tried to pretend like everything was normal—which is hard to do when you are awaiting surgery. Trying to get her to relax and laugh a little—I asked the hospital staff, "Do you mind if I assist in the operating room?" A puzzled nurse inquired, "You know anything about surgery?" "No," said I, "but I did stay at a Holiday Inn Express last night."

Yes, commercials capture our attention and tickle our funny bones —even in tense moments. Sometimes, that's okay.

Christmas Lights

I've had it with my neighbors. Each Christmas season they put out more holiday stuff in their yards and more lights on their houses than the year before. But that isn't the annoying part. The worst part is that they do it earlier each year. And my wife notices.

"Do you see that?" she asks, "We need to get one of those." Or "Would you just look at those icicle lights, they are beautiful..." Or "Let's buy one of those white reindeer..." I know from experience what's coming: another trip to the hardware store for more lights, more stuff, and more extension cords. (I haven't measured, but I think we have enough orange extension cord to go from here to the moon—or at least to Murfreesboro!)

One year we even outlined our fence row in lights. I lived in fear that a 737 pilot might mistake my pasture for Nashville International.

All of which brings me back to my original thought. Christmas seems to come earlier each year. I'm putting away the fake pumpkins on the *same day* my wife is hanging garland. What gives? And we *never* put up our tree while the calendar still says "November." But we're getting close. And get this: if you want a decent parking space at the mall to do some Christmas shopping, I suggest you start looking in ... *August*

And have you noticed that there is always one family on the street who leave their lights up year 'round? We always made fun of them. Hmm. Maybe they are smarter than we thought.

Now before you pass judgment that I must be the reincarnation of Ebenezer Scrooge, please be advised that I love this season of the year. I delight in giving and seeing smiles stretch across innocent faces. I enjoy the "I'm not so sure this is a good idea" look of uncertainty as children are coaxed by parents to sit on Santa's lap. (I also wonder if the guy in red is really thinking, "Aren't you getting a little big for this?" when sat upon by a good size third grader.) But it's a delightful time of the year when we sing carols, exchange cards, and drink eggnog (I know. I hate eggnog, too).

From our family to yours: Have a wonderful holiday season! And if you happen to see a beleaguered looking fellow leaving the hardware store with a bundle on his back, it's not Santa's helper; it's me. And it's not a bundle of toys; it's more extension cord.

I'm the Greatest!

With an apology for sounding like a swaggering Muhammed Ali, I wish to boast about a personal achievement that deserves some measure of public recognition. In other words, if no one else will toot my horn, I will.

It is my humble opinion that I have been blessed with a unique ability that transcends all others. In fact, I have taken this natural gift and, through the years, perfected it into an art. Others may claim equality with my talent but to this day I have never met my equal. Never.

I am the greatest ... *at finding a way to get in the wrong line.*

It's true. If they gave gold medals for people standing in lines that long ago stopped moving, I would have a trophy room full of hardware. It never fails. For example, if you see me driving in the far right lane of I-65 (some people think I'm "far right" most of the time ...), do yourself a great big favor and *get in the other lane.* My lane will stop. Guaranteed.

My wife once sent me into a Mississippi McDonalds late one night for a simple cup of coffee. No problem. Fact is: there was no line because there were no people. Not even I could mess that up. After politely asking, "May I hep ya?" (they say "hep" a lot down there) and taking my money, the young girl turned and began the excruciating slow and painful process of making the coffee. And do you think that at some point she could stop the event and pour me a quick cup? Nope. She waited and waited *and waited* until every drop filled the pot. I'm the only one who can get in a wrong line when there isn't one.

Then there was the time I ran into a Memphis Wal-Mart to grab some hairspray for my grandmother—a simple single item to be purchased with *cash.* Out of twenty lanes of choice, I made a calculated gamble and chose the "Cash Only— Eight Items or Less" line. There was only one person ahead of me—a harmless looking elderly lady. That harmless looking senior citizen became entangled in a hopeless argument with the cashier over the cost of two lousy couch pillows. "No," the older customer declared, "these pillows are on sale for $2.99 and I won't pay a penny more!" Great. Then proceeded the circus of looking through store mail-out circulars, a conversation with the manager, further discussions ad infinitum. The lady left that Wal-Mart purchasing those pillows for $2.99. I know because I paid the difference. Why not? I would still be there if I hadn't.

I won't bore you with other details of my success—after all, there is something nauseating about people who brag. But sometimes, like Ali, you stake your claim to fame and challenge all comers.

Consider yourself duly warned.

It's All About the Kids

I sat in a room the other night with a group of twenty-, thirty-, and a few of us forty-something year-old guys—and participated in a draft for the upcoming local Dixie Youth Baseball 7-8 year-old season. It was fun. It was fun because the guys coaching made it fun. It was fun because of the anticipation of the upcoming season. It was fun because of the kids.

Sometimes we forget what it's all about. And what it is all about is ... the kids.

I am a *big* baseball fan—always have been. I remember as a teenager the weekend New York Yankee pitcher, Lindy McDaniel, stayed in our home and slept in my bed. A major league ballplayer stayed in my room! Can you believe that? (I refused to let my mother wash the sheets for a month!) I also have a signed baseball by Hall of Famer, Stan "The Man" Musial (it's *not* for sale!). And I have a treasure-chest of memories ranging from visits to Cooperstown to sitting in the stands of major and minor league ballparks all over the country. And in the summer of '91, I did one of the craziest things ever—I drove twelve hours with my oldest son so we could play baseball one hot July afternoon in the middle of an Iowa cornfield made famous by Kevin Costner's Field of Dreams.

I am a *big* baseball fan.

Nothing, however, compares with the atmosphere of little league baseball. Nothing.

There is something special about seeing a youngster finally get it. Hitting a small round ball with a bat is a big part of a little boy's rite of passage. Getting a hit in the bottom of the last inning and scoring the winning run is what little boys dream about. It's why they wear baseball caps and fall asleep with their baseball gloves. And... it's why they stand all alone in the backyard, throw a ball up into the air, and take on the voice of the P.A. announcer, "Now batting, Derek Jeter..."

It's all about the kids.

Some guys don't get it. Sometimes egos get in the way and winning becomes everything. Sure, everyone likes winning better than losing but the real winners may be the coaches who can lose with class and teach their kids to do the same. Those youngsters will grow up one day and be introduced to a life of disappointments. Baseball, then, becomes a microcosm of what is to come. To some it is just a silly game. But to a few, it is an opportunity to teach about something far greater.

I was impressed with these guys. They get it. It's all about the kids.

My Favorite

This is by far my favorite season of the year. There is a "feel" about it, a distinct and undeniable aura that surrounds this particular season. Hot, humid days and sweltering summer nights are replaced by cool, crisp mornings. The pleasant afternoon breezes will soon loosen the leaves, creating a blanket for the yard in preparation for colder days to come. And somehow hot cider tastes best on a cool autumn night.

I'm looking forward to frost on the pumpkins. The Canadian geese, flying in their famed V-formation, are beginning to make their way to warmer climates, neighbors are busy stacking firewood, and Friday night gridiron action takes on an added dimension as teams battle and bands play.

It's fall, yaw'll.

I love this time of year, don't you? Yes, I know it's a monster of a time for those who suffer from allergies—but that's what all the expensive medicine is for. *(Warn-*

ing: Don't be like a friend of mine who was taking the allergy medication Allegra only to get confused about the name and in a *very loud* voice announced to everyone in the church foyer that... "Now that I'm on *Viagra*—all of my problems are solved." Hmm.)

Now where was I? Ah, yes, fall. What a wonderful time for reflection and evaluation, for slowing the pace and rethinking motives, for counting blessings and renewing commitments. This season of the year, perhaps more than any other, helps me remember that:

- there is more fun to be had in giving than taking;
- there is more to be learned by listening than talking;
- there is greater reward in life's little things than in the big stuff.

Slow down a little this fall and celebrate the seasonal change by reflecting on God's grace and goodness and, at the same time, enjoy some quality moments with family and friends. Around my house we call it "making a memory" and there are a lot of memories to be made this time of year.

Seasons change but God remains constant. That's good to remember since the beauty of autumn will soon be replaced by the icy blasts of winter. But, you know, you can count on God then, too. Enjoy!

Old Blue

If you've ever loved an old dog...

We called him "Old Blue." We're not sure how old he was when he came to join us, but my tender-hearted wife could not bear the thought of seeing this full-bred, blue-eyed, senior citizen Border Collie live out his remaining days at the pound. And so with her permission, Old Blue jumped into the van and headed for his new home in the country.

He was old but still strong. As soon as he spotted our barn and family of goats, those herding instincts returned and on every occasion Old Blue loved to do what he did best: herd. It was amazing to watch him work. He was so intent on encircling the flock and getting them into the barn that nothing else mattered. And when the job was done, he looked up as if to say, "Pretty good, huh?"—then together we would head to the house for a special reward.

Old Blue was smart. He loved to shake hands—at least shake your hand and his big paw. He loved children, got along amicably with our other pets, and preferred not to bark for much of anything. Then again, maybe that's because Old Blue was deaf. He couldn't hear worth a lick but that handicap never seemed to bother him, for once he saw you his tail would go into motion and he would sit up with paw extended.

We could tell that Blue was growing older and slower. The day came when he would stand at the fence and watch the goats rather than head to the field to herd. In his later and sicker days he traded goats for trucks, preferring to herd the UPS truck or any other truck that ventured onto our place. Old Blue would crouch low; focus his eyes and circle–doing his best to get that big brown truck into the barn. Of course, he never did but he sure gave it everything he had.

In the final weeks he began losing a lot of weight. He stopped eating, his eyes grew cloudy and we discovered lumps that we figured were cancerous. We did our best to keep him as comfortable as possible for as long as possible.

Finally, we did a tough but loving thing. We had him put to sleep. If you've ever done that, then you know how hard it is. The doctor confirmed our fears that there was nothing more we could do for Old Blue. As she prepared the injection, Old Blue lifted up his head and raised his paw. He wanted to shake one more time. We think it was his way of saying "thank you."

Our big yard seems especially empty these days and I catch myself looking for him when I pull into the drive or walk out to the barn. As long as I live, I'll never forget Old Blue. And ... something tells me that the UPS man will remember him, too.

Late Night Latté

I saw this startling statistic the other day—a survey reported that the average American couple spends twelve minutes per week in eye-to-eye communication. Not per day – per week! That's absurd. But sadly, it's probably true.

There are a lot of contributing factors to that statistic—busyness, selfishness, too many hobbies, dual-income families, sports, television, exhaustion, etc., but regardless of our 21st century age of overloaded lives we must somehow and some way get communication back into our homes. We must learn to look at one another and talk about the stuff that really matters.

And *both* sexes are at fault. Guys, I'm talking about real in-depth—put the paper down and turn off ESPN—and listen. Women, I'm talking about understanding a simple single *fact of life:* the age of miracles is over—we cannot read your mind! It is said that the three most feared words to a man are: "Honey, let's talk!" It's true—because the male creature by nature is a fixer and not a talker. But guys, most of the times she doesn't want you to "fix" her problem but to simply listen. And ladies, you must do two things: (1) pick your moments and (2) be patient.

Each night my wife and I have a standing date—after the kids are down and things get quiet, she makes a pot of coffee and we rendezvous at the kitchen table and talk about our day—our work, the kids, people we can encourage, our finances, personal problems, things we need to do, difficult decisions, etc. It is an investment in our relationship that has returned multiple dividends. Strangely enough, a very funny thing happened around that kitchen table. Over the years we talked so long and sampled so many different kinds of flavored coffees that we decided to open a coffee shop. (So we did!)

Twelve minutes per week in eye-to-eye communication... We've got to do better than that. It starts in your home. With you. Now. And by the way, if you need a good brew of flavored coffee to get the ball rolling, we will be happy to make a recommendation. It comes from years of personal experience.

I'm Middle-Age...
But Only If I Live To Be 94

Today is my birthday. I think. You see, you only know it's your birthday because that's what other people tell you. It's certainly not like you remember much about that day—come to think of it, you don't remember much about the first several hundred days. Life is funny like that. You struggle with memory the first few years of life and then, at the end, the memory bug bites you again. Somewhere in between, you live and remember who you are and where you live. Hopefully.

I think this is my birthday because I have an official piece of paper from the government stating that it is my birthday. And the government is 100% right most of the time.

If this is my birthday, and I have every reason to believe that it is, then I am forty-seven years old. That used to seem very old to me. Fact is, thirty used to seem old to me. It doesn't any more. But neither does forty or fifty. Sixty is even looking younger all the time. I used to think that only elderly people retired but it looks to me as if the sixty-something crowd is retiring earlier than ever before.

Someone said that I am "middle age." That may be true

but only if I live to be ninety-four. I hope I live to be ninety-four, in fact, I hope I live to be one hundred and four. I have this theory that the odds of dying go down the longer you live. I don't see many obituaries from people once they pass the century mark. Do you?

Speaking of obituaries...I remember that my grandmother used to read them every day. I always thought that was the section of paper devoted to grandparent people so they could check and see whether or not they made the list. Kind of like when final test grades used to be posted outside the classroom door. I think those were the days before the privacy act.

You would think the privacy act would apply to obituaries. Great, now I'm dead and everyone knows it. I'm surprised someone hasn't sued over that.

Speaking of being dead... Here is something that I don't understand. Explain to me why you spend your entire life waiting at red lights but when you're dead, they put you in a Cadillac station wagon and run every one of them. I guess when you're dead it's important to make good time.

I was eating very bland oatmeal this morning when a friend phoned to wish me a happy birthday. She informed me that I should count my blessings because when I'm fifty-something, my diet will consist of shredded (make that "dreaded") wheat. Something to do with regularity. And when I'm sixty-something, I'll move on to Grape Nuts and become fixated with regularity and even talk about it publicly. I can't wait.

Today is my birthday. I'm one-half of ninety-four. Pass the Dreaded Wheat.

Miracle Salve and TV Lawyers

I was sick. I came down with a "respiratory disorder" (meaning I coughed and moaned a lot) and spent most of the day as a couch potato seeking solace in that wonderful medium of cable nostalgia called *TV Land*. You know, the channel that shows all the old TV programs–back when writers could write funny scripts without profanity or sex. No kidding.

I have forgotten how entertaining the old black and white *I Love Lucy* or *Dick Van Dyke* shows were in the 60s or... how silly *Green Acres* was in the 70s or... how bad the acting was in some of the cop shows of the 80s. I decided something else, too–it's better to be sick today than then. Back then, the only daytime TV programming that passed the time were Game Shows and Soap Operas. Not exactly motivation for skipping school and feigning illness.

The commercials, however, make the most impact. Commercial advertising on daytime television today falls into two main categories: (1) ads from pharmaceutical companies encouraging you to "ask your doctor" for their latest miracle drug, and (2) ads from lawyers asking if you have been incapacitated from the side effects of pharmaceutical drugs. Call 1-800-SUE-THEM.

I filled a prescription for a couple of those "miracle" drugs. After forking out $250 for a steroid inhaler and a month supply of "Sing-u-lair" (they advertise that on TV, too—they just don't tell you how much it costs), I was armed with the needed ammunition to bounce back. My wife, however, was armed with a remedy of her own. You might even say it was right under her nose. Or mine.

Vick's Salve. Her homespun recipe for respiratory distress consists of the following:

1. Boil water
2. Drop in a big glob of Vick's Salve
3. Drape towel over husband's head and stick his face very near the pan for as long as he can stand it
4. Stand over him and make him "stand it" a little longer than reasonable
5. When husband lifts head, force down again with hand

It works. Now that I think of it, my grandmother used that stuff all the time. She believed Vick's Salve was the miracle drug that could cure anything. Broken leg? No problem. Rub on some Vick's Salve and off you go. Maybe that's why her bedroom always smelled like menthol.

As the pharmaceutical ads warn, however, there are side effects to any medication. Stick your head in a hot pot of Vick's Salve and there will be some side effects. Your congestion will loosen and you will breath much better, for sure, but...your eyes will water and sting like crazy and your neck will hurt from being forced to bend over so long.

The side effects will eventually go away. But if not, there seem to be plenty of TV lawyers waiting to help.

Green Bananas

My grandmother, *bless her heart* ("bless her heart" is what you say when you're from the South and speak in reference to your grandmother), always knew she was going to die just any day. In fact, she warned us regularly about her impending demise every time we would leave after a visit. "Well," she would begin, "this is the last time you'll ever see Nana... I'm getting old and won't be around much longer..." I remember her saying that when I was in grade school, in middle school, high school and college. She kept on saying it in the years that followed. She always knew she would die.

And she did.

My grandmother, the one who thought she was going to die any day—was born in 1906 and lived to see the 21st century! The fact is: she outlived most everyone else in the family. A few years back when she was in her mid-eighties and running around with friends much younger than she, I asked why she didn't hang out with those her own age. "Son," she said, "most people my age are in the cemetery and many of those who aren't, ought to be." Nana was blunt. Maybe that was her secret.

Some folks are so pessimistic about not living to see another day that they actually alter their lifestyle. A friend told me recently about an older lady he knows who refuses to buy green bananas—"May not be around long enough to eat them" was her rationale. And I heard just last week about an older man who buys milk only by the half-gallon. "No need to waste money on what I won't live to use." Of course, he buys two half-gallons at a time...

All of which brings me back to my grandmother. In 1972, she bought a new Oldsmobile. "I bought a new one 'cause it's the last car I'll ever have..." Guess what? She was right. It *was* the last car she would ever have—mainly because she drove it only three times per week (prayer-meeting on Wednesday, beauty shop on Friday, and church on Sunday). But that was my grandmother, always thinking ahead and planning to die. It just happened a lot later than she predicted.

Come to think of it, she didn't buy green bananas either. *Bless her heart.*

Life Stinks (Sometimes)

There was no way to stop her. When a young Golden Retriever spots a cat, all the discipline in the world goes out the window. Something called "natural instinct" kicks in and the chase is on. Only this time the pretty little kitty with the white stripe down its back didn't budge. She held her ground and demanded R•E•S•P•E•C•T. She got it.

And man's best friend came home with her tail tucked between her legs and a very distinct and non-desirable aroma.

What to do with a dog that has been "skunked?" I've heard the old tomato juice theory but we did something a little different. Read on.

All of which reminded me of a true story in which a mother once returned from the store, walked into the living room and saw her five children huddled together and concentrating with intense interest on an object they had cornered. When she discovered the center of their attention, she could not believe her eyes. Smack dab in the middle of the circle were several baby skunks. She dropped her groceries and screamed at the top of her voice: "Children run!" They did. Each child grabbed a baby skunk and took off!

Life can get complicated.

Everyone has days when life just plain stinks. Things go wrong, people disappoint us, criticism and comments begin to take their toll, circumstances beat us down to the ground until we're just weary and worn out to a frazzle. Now I'm all for looking on the bright side but I also know a little about reality–and reality says that some days you feel as if you've been "skunked." And it stinks.

You know what I think? I think you've been there. I know you've been there because I've been there. But here is the *good news*–you don't have to stay there! You *can* pick yourself up and, by the grace of God, find the strength to face another day. Remember the old saying, "There is nothing that can happen that the Lord and I can't face together." Or something like that. Anyway, it's true.

So the next time you have a day that "stinks"–just take a long, soaking bath in tomato juice or whatever relieves the smell –and then go do something good and constructive. And smile. Nothing takes away the stink of a bad day more than a positive attitude.

Oh yes, we found a new de-skunk remedy via the Internet. Are you ready? Here it is: Massengill douche! No, I'm not kidding. Besides, it sure beats trying to get a nervous Golden Retriever to stay in a tub of tomato juice...

Backpacks and Heartaches

My heart aches for my friend. David, a well-respected attorney in a nearby city, knows all too well the agonizing pain of grief and how quickly life can go from calm to chaos. His beautiful wife of thirty years passed away last week. Suddenly. There was no warning or hint that anything was amiss. A phone call in the morning was perfectly normal while the call that came that afternoon was anything but.

It's amazing how quickly life can turn upside down.

There are no words to describe this level of grief. Some of you know because you have been there and walked down a similar path. What you don't know is that this isn't the first time my friend has faced life's deepest pain. As we talked last Friday evening over supper, he said, "You know, I have found myself saying, 'It's me...*again*, Lord.'"

It was nearly five years ago that this family received the dreaded phone message that their oldest son had been killed in a tragic highway accident. He was on his way back to college in Indiana when his life ended abruptly. Some say that time heals all wounds. Those who say that have never buried a child.

I remember so vividly hiking with David and other friends last fall in the back country of Montana's Glacier National Park. We had put a couple of miles behind us on what was a beautiful day in the Rockies not far from the Canadian border. As we walked he talked–about his beloved son and the pain of his grief. At some point along the wooded trail, he could go no further. He stopped and wept quietly. We all did. Backpacks hit the ground as a group of grown men shared a few quiet moments of compassion for one who was hurting so deeply. After a few moments of rest, we wiped our eyes, strapped on our packs, and continued the silent journey.

My friend will have to strap on his pack again. This time, however, his life-load will be heavier than ever before.

There are some things for which I do not have an answer. No one does. The seeming randomness of suffering will always remain a mystery. The fact that some people appear to breeze through life without so much as a speed bump and others find themselves continually bruised and bleeding on the rocks of grief is beyond my ability to understand. I cannot answer the "Why" question–neither can you. But I do know that there are life-lessons only to be learned in the depths of despair. And...I know this: grace is only meaningful to those who need it.

My heart aches for my friend.

Church Can Be Funny

I don't mean to sound sacrilegious, but funny things do happen at church. Sometimes I have to just stop and smile.

Like the lady who quit listening to me and started watching a bee buzzing around a good brother's head. The bee decided to land on top and she, without a lot of contemplative thought, decided to whack it with the Good Book. She missed!—the bee...not the head.

There was the time I was five minutes into a lesson on "Procrastination" when I noticed an older man slumping over in obvious pain. He was having a heart attack, which made it imperative that we stop the proceedings. The situation shook everyone up so bad that when we were finally able to resume the service, it was no use. So I made this impromptu announcement: "Due to what we have just experienced, my sermon on Procrastination will be put off until next week..." The fellow ended up fine and I never did get around to preaching that sermon.

Then there was the time I sat behind the cutest little girl singing joyful hymns to the Lord. We were singing, "Bringing in the Sheaves" while she, on the other hand, was singing loudly, "Bringing in the Cheese."

It broke up the place one Sunday when a father decided to discipline his misbehaving five-year-old. Rather than taking him out the back, he proceeded to throw him over his shoulder and walk toward the front where he would quickly and quietly duck out a side door. Wrong. About the time father and son reached the front, the little boy looked back at the Sunday worshippers and pleaded passionately—"Pray for me!" I'm not sure anyone remembered the sermon that day, but that kid will live in infamy.

A little boy was playing with his cars on the front row when the preacher said, "Son, you need to stop that." He did—but not before he made an ear-splitting, tire screeching sound to indicate that his car had come to a complete stop.

I wasn't there, but those who were will never forget the day someone was baptized by a fellow who had never done that before. A quick-thinking brother handed him a handkerchief to use in the baptism that could cover the responder's mouth and nose. Of course, the brother never told him that. Thus, when the curtain opened there stood the poor fellow being baptized wearing a handkerchief around nose and mouth, tied in the back, and looking for all the world like Jesse James robbing a bank.

Yes, "there is a time to laugh..."—even in church.

It's All In a Name

I grew up, for the most part, in Kentucky. I have always held a unique fondness for our northern neighbor–for bluegrass and basketball, horse farms and happy times. Yes, I know all the "briar" jokes (usually told by Indiana friends–which reminds me... just what is a "Hoosier" anyway?) and of course the on-going rivalry between Wildcats and Volunteers. *Just wait till basketball season!*

One thing that has always amazed (and amused!) me about My Old Kentucky Home is this: where did they get the names for the towns? There must be a "story" behind each one, whether folklore or real, but you must admit that Kentuckians get an "A" for road-map creativity.

All aboard for a bluegrass back roads tour...

They like animals in Kentucky. Not only are they the only state with a *"Horse Cave"* but they also have such notables such as *"Monkeys Eyebrow,"* and *"Rooster Run,"* and *"Dog Walk."* Did you know that *"Happy"* is not far from *"Rowdy?"*–and *"Beauty"* is only a hop-skip-and-a-jump from *"Lovely?"* (I am *not* making this up.)

Some towns bespeak southern charm and hospitality, such as: *"Do Stop"* and *"Stopover."* Beware of *"Quicksand"* which is close to *"Shoulderblade"*—which I am sure involves some kind of connecting tale. Someone with a sense of humor must have named (and misspelled) *"Mummie"* which is only five miles down the road from *"Egypt."*

Speaking of foreign countries, *"Canada," "Sweden,"* and *"Cuba"* are all a lot closer than you think they are. And international cities, too. I read that during World War II, a local resident took up arms when he heard that Nazi forces were marching on *"Warsaw."* Maybe he should have checked with *"London."* Then again, I heard there was much confusion up the road in *"Baghdad."*

I remember riding in the backseat with my younger brother years ago as our parents drove up highway 31-E somewhere north of Glasgow. He said, "Where are we?" I answered, *"Uno."* "No really," he asked, "Where are we?" I said, *"Uno!"* "No, I *don't* know," he added with a grin. Our little "who's on first" routine went on until my father had had enough (which didn't take too long). *Uno, Kentucky.* You gotta love it.

You think I'm pulling your leg? Get a map. In the meantime, while you're trying to get it unfolded, I think I'll head up *"Fruit Hill"* and see if I can find a *"Honeybee."* Or maybe make my way up to *"Windy Hill"* and pick up a *"Thousand Sticks."* It never ends.

Some might think I'm from *"Preachersville,"* but I'm not. I'm from *"Shepherdsville."* Funny thing, I never knew any preachers from "Preachersville" nor did I ever see any shepherds around Shepherdsville. But that's Kentucky... and my beloved home.

Snow Day!

It strikes glee in the heart of every child and fear in the heart of every parent.

What child hasn't sprung from their bed and thrown open the sash—well, okay, maybe the blinds—and jumped for joy at the surprise of white? And what parent hasn't cringed at the first sighting of Snow Bird, or Snow Hound, or whatever abominable snow creature lists the school closings (along with that *very annoying* jingle that goes with it)?

Snow day! You know what I think? I don't think our kids get that excited about all the national Monday holidays named after really old people. You expect those. You know what gives kids an off-the-wall, parental headache-splitting high? *Snow day!* There is nothing in life that compares. Nothing.

A snow day means everything to a kid. It's a day of celebration; it's the real Independence Day. It's Christmas and New Year's and Thanksgiving–especially "Thanksgiving"–all rolled into one. Ask a forty-something businessman about his favorite snow-day memories and watch the frown disappear and his childhood return. Snow days are special.

My heart goes out to kids from Florida. They may have the Magic Kingdom but they miss out on the most magical day of all.

Snow day! It's a couple extra hours of the best sleep you have ever had. It's pancakes and real maple syrup (not the "Lite" diet stuff). It's a snowball fight with your brother. It's a water-dripping pile of soggy hats, gloves, socks and shoes on the kitchen floor. It's hot cocoa and rosy red cheeks. It's afternoon movie rentals and popcorn on the couch. It's all of that and more.

I have discovered that you don't even need snow to have a "snow day." Schools around these parts have been known to call off education for a day due to a forecast that never happened or for a snow they didn't exactly need a yardstick to measure. A few flakes? Hmm. Better to be safe than sorry. By the way, the superintendent was a kid once. He knows.

So the next time there is a "snow day"–enjoy! It's okay. Make those pancakes (remember: *real* maple syrup!), throw a snowball, pour some hot chocolate, and...be a kid again. After all, they will be back in school tomorrow.

I hope...

Edith

I'll call her Edith (the name has been changed to protect the embarrassed). My older friend recently experienced one of life's greatest fears—the kind of phobia that haunts many an elderly person who would dare to venture out into the wild unknown that we commonly call—the Mall.

Edith lost her car.

She couldn't remember where she had parked. She was so preoccupied with her shopping excursion (making a list and checking it twice) that when she emerged from the great spending-charging jungle of American commerce, she had not the slightest idea where it was. Before her lay a frightening sea of four-wheel transportation that seemed to disappear into the horizon.

Fortunately for her (and unfortunately for him), a kind and gentle mall security vehicle happened along. Upon explaining her dilemma, the young officer was all too eager to assist. He drove Edith up one row and down another. No car. He drove her to another parking lot—you know, one the size of Rhode Island—no car. He drove around and around for nearly an hour while listening to her wonderful stories about family and friends and recent visits to the doctor's office. No car.

Then finally (and after some hard praying on his part), he found it. And that's when the real trouble began.

Edith discovered that she had locked her keys in the car. That's right. There they were—plain as anyone could see—sitting in the ignition. The kind and gentle man muttered something under his breath while figuring out a way to retrieve the keys. Nothing worked. He called for backup (I don't know the code for "officer in distress" but I am sure that he used it). But it was no use. Edith had two options: call for a locksmith and pay an outrageous sum, or the security officer could break a small side window and she could gain immediate entrance. Edith chose the latter.

They broke the window.

And that's when Edith discovered something else that was quite amazing—it wasn't her car!

Maybe it was the keys she "discovered" in the bottom of her purse that gave it away. Or maybe it was the fact that Buicks and Oldsmobiles look remarkably similar. Whatever it was, Edith was thrilled to learn that she hadn't locked the keys in her car after all. And now, she wanted to know, would the kind security man mind driving her around again since she was pretty certain she left her car close to J.C. Penney.

I don't know whatever happened to the security officer (I think he took an early retirement—a medical discharge?) nor do I know what happened to the poor fellow who discovered that his Buick had been vandalized by mall security—but I do know this: Edith is...Edith. And is still on the loose.

Grits

You have to be from the South to enjoy them. There is just something special about a bowl of piping hot grits with melted butter—a little salt and a lot of pepper—to get you going on a cool autumn morning. And when those grits are coupled with a thick slice of salty country ham (not city ham!), and a good cup of steaming coffee, well, there can't be a much better way to jump-start your day.

It reminds me of a true story I heard about a fellow from Michigan who ordered breakfast during a recent jaunt into the Deep South. He saw grits on the menu, and since he had spent his entire life on the northern side of the Mason-Dixon, he wasn't very clear on the nature of this southern delicacy. So he informed the waitress, "I've never had grits and don't know even if I would like them." "So," he continued, "better just bring me one."

Her response was classic. "Honey," she said (it's written some where in Confederate Law that waitresses in the South address their male patrons as "Honey"), "grits don't come by themselves."

It's true. Grits don't exist in isolation. In fact, a great philosopher once said, "No grit is an island." You can't order one grit. It's sort of a package deal.

It's the same with people.

God never intended for people to live in isolation. That's why God said, "It is not good for man to be alone." That's why we have families...and churches... and communities...—because we need other people. Honey, you don't come by yourself.

There is a special longing in the human heart to connect, to love and be loved. From the smallest child who lifts up her little arms in the hopes of being held, to my widower friend who remarried when nearly eighty (the last time he dated, Harry Truman was President!)—people need people. Someone once said, "As frustrating as people can be, it's hard to find a good substitute." It's true.

It's not about me. I wasn't put here on this earth to please and amuse myself. I am part of the grits. I am a husband, father, father-in-law, brother, uncle, friend, neighbor, etc. And so are you. You are part of the grits. And, honey, we don't come by ourselves.

Think about that the next time you order a bowl of this southern staple. Grits just work better when they're bunched together. It's the same with people.

Appalachian Memories

The foreboding backcountry of the Appalachian Mountains has always intrigued me. The hills and hollows reveal a world completely foreign to most of us. The Loretta Lynn story of a coal miner's daughter growing up in poverty stricken Butcher Hollow can be repeated thousands of times. Daniel Boone once described the Appalachians as "so wild...that it is impossible to behold them without terror." Times have changed since the days of Boone and his clashes with Indians, but the stories of the hills—of the Hatfield's and McCoy's, moonshine and revenuers, black lung and poverty are probably truer than we know.

I had lunch yesterday with a delightful family who live up Coon Creek. They have several acres of mountain land that rises abruptly from the back porch. Backyards as we know them are rare in mountain communities. I have heard that mountain livestock have two legs longer than the others providing for greater balance—but I think someone was pulling *my* leg.

Once I performed a wedding ceremony in the border town of Bluefield and stayed in a mountain home that was built next to a very sharp curve on the Norfolk and Western railroad track. There is nothing quite like being awakened from sleep in the middle of the night by the light of a locomotive headlamp flooding the room and the sense of sheer panic at what seems like an eerie one-sided game of chicken with a two hundred ton coal train. Fortunately, he swerved first.

This was the same mountain house that had the most peculiar appliance ever invented—a gas-fired toilet. I did discover one advantage to a natural gas commode (no jokes, please)—the seat is always warm. Always. But...I would highly recommend you flush while in the standing position.

I have found the people of Appalachia to be absolutely engaging and hospitable. Their world has been expanded from what it used to be, thanks to new four-lane highways and satellite television. But in other ways, it is still a culture all to its own. And truthfully, mountain people prefer that it remain such.

Then again, much of the world has come to the front porch of these mountains through the toe-tappin' Bluegrass music made popular by mountain men like Ralph Stanley. Stanley is a living legend in the hills and yet he has always been a humble man of the mountains. He, like so many others, is one with his people.

Appalachia is a unique place in a diverse country of cultures. The mountain folk are proud to call it home. They should be.

Business As (Almost) Usual

The threat level goes up and down. News reports warn of possible terrorist plans to disrupt our normalcy; flights are cancelled; major cities are on a heightened state of alert. Code *orange*. There is a tinge of fear in the air. And given the events of recent past, it is not unfounded.

Fear. It is something we are going to have to face head on and conquer. To do otherwise is to give terrorism the victory and hand them even further incentive to inflict additional deeds of destruction. It doesn't mean that we fail to be cognizant of potential danger nor spit in the face of common sense, but it does mean that we get on with our lives.

No, we won't forget the events of that horrific day. September 11, 2001 will be burned forever into our collective psyche. Nor does it mean that we sacrifice America's renewed national spirit for a return to the former habits of patriotic passivity. Patriotism and life as (almost) usual are not mutually exclusive. They can co-exist and *must* co-exist. Especially now.

So...keep those flags flying. That is especially important as many of us have friends and family serving in the military. I have a good friend who just returned from Baghdad. We gave him a hero's welcome home. He deserved it. So does every soldier who serves his country in time of war.

And yet we must continue on with our lives. Our children and families need to see courage and bravery replace anxiety and fear. Somehow our faith level must rise above our fear level. Our kids need to see us pray for our country and then see us trust the God in whom we say we believe.

I go to the airport and get on an airplane. I attend sporting events. I shop at the mall. There is no nut case in Iraq or Afghanistan (okay, I said it!) that is going to stop me from living my life. Cautious? Sure. Paranoid? No way. Determined? You bet. *God bless America! And God bless our bravest who help to bring freedom to people who have never known it.*

Letters to God

I am surrounded in my office by all kinds of books—big books, important books, substantial books of scholarly information containing big words and lots of serious stuff. But among the hundreds of volumes in my library, my all-time favorite is a pocket-sized book called *Children's Letters to God* by Stuart Hample and Eric Marshall. It is exactly what it says it is—a simple collection of crayon and pencil writings from children to God.

This little book puts everything into perspective. A few excerpts to make you smile:

Dear God, I went to this wedding and they kissed right in church. Is that ok?

Neil

Dear God, Thank you for the baby brother but what I prayed for was a puppy.

Joyce

Dear God, Maybe Cain and Abel would not kill each other so much if they had their own rooms. It works with my brother.

Larry

Dear God, I bet it is very hard for you to love all of everybody in the whole world. There are only 4 people in our family and I can never do it.

Nan

Dear God, Please send Dennis Clark to a different camp this year.

Peter

Dear God, My grandpa says you were around when he was a little boy. How far back do you go?

Dennis

Dear God, I didn't think orange went with purple until I saw the sunset you made on Tuesday. That was cool.

Eugene

Dear God, I am doing the best I can.

Frank

(Me, too, Frank.)

It's More Than a Game

Busch Stadium in St. Louis sits next to the famous Gateway Arch and just a few hundred yards west of the Mississippi River. It is home to the National League St. Louis Cardinals. And it's a long way from my home—307 miles for those wishing to be exact.

Driving to a baseball game in Missouri was the farthest thing from my mind as I waited in line at the bank that Monday morning. Sure, it was a day off work and the kids were out of school and we wanted to do something together as a family... (I think a nice breakfast outing was more in line with my wife's idea.) But then I saw it. The St. Louis Cardinals were hosting the Cincinnati Reds in a night game at Busch. I could think of a hundred reasons why the mere suggestion would be ridiculous. Driving to Missouri and back on the same day... The cost of gas... The late return... Work on Tuesday... I mean, let's be sensible, right?

Sometimes sensibility has to take a back seat to spontaneity. Besides, this is summer (well, almost!) and the keynote of an American summer is baseball.

Baseball. Baseball is more than a game—it is a pastime. Theme parks can be fun but older kids scatter quickly and prefer "hanging" with friends rather than parents. Let's face it, family togetherness doesn't exactly happen at theme parks. But it does happen at national parks—the kind with grass, bleachers, hot dogs, and Cracker Jacks.

Baseball. Take your family to a ballgame and you will be together as a family. You will sit together and yell together and eat together. Especially that last part.

Baseball. It's brilliant green grass set in contrast to a dazzling blue sky. It's the seventh inning stretch, scorecards and the smell of a ballpark. It's youngsters holding out a baseball glove and hoping for the ultimate souvenir. It's Jeter, and Sosa, and Griffey. It's introducing your kids to a non-video version of America's greatest game.

307 miles seems like a long way to drive to go to a ballgame. I guess it is if that's all there is to it. But as we walked out of Busch Stadium, a weary little leaguer held my hand and said, "Dad, thank you so much for taking me to this ballgame; you're the greatest."

I may never have the adulation of the greats of Cooperstown but for one night I was an All-Star where it matters most.

Just Ordinary

My college-age son and I travel each summer from our White House home to the Great Smoky Mountains National Park in our quest to conquer 6593-foot Mt. LeConte. It's hardly a pleasure stroll to LeConte's rocky top summit but once you've made it, you know the thrill of a hiker's high.

I have never been to the mountain when I was not filled with a sense of awe and respect for the creation of God. I have never been to the mountain when I did not come away refreshed in my soul and appreciative of the simple things in life. Mountain top vistas slowly put the daily hassles of life back into perspective. Father and son talks somehow take on additional meaning when hiking above the clouds. And people you meet along the trail seem a little nicer and more conversational than those you encounter on crowded city streets.

But not every day is a mountain top experience. The fact is that most of us live on the level land of the ordinary. We have to go to the grocery store and post office and pharmacy. We sit at red lights and wait in traffic lines. Yes, most of the time we engage in the mundane "stuff" of ordinary every day living.

That's life.

So smile. And while you're at it... take a moment to hold the door for the young mom with two kids in tow... be extra kind to a teenager working behind the counter at a fast food restaurant... thank a police officer for caring... compliment an elderly person... help a neighbor... tip a little extra... gripe a little less... help a little more.

After all, we're all on the trail together.

Whatever Happened to...Manners?

My wife is a stickler for two things—the proper use of the English language and...*manners.* She cringes when she hears someone say, "I'm going to lay down..." or "I ain't got no..." or "Me and him went..." (Makes you wonder if they still teach English grammar in school...) But back to *manners.* (Yes, I know—that is a fragmented sentence.)

Manners are defined as "polite ways of social behavior." It's that "polite" part that is usually "missing in action." Politeness and deference to others seems foreign in a society that gravitates toward selfishness and me-first. The basis of manners, however, is recognition that other people are important, too.

When we gather around the family table for supper (and, yes, we eat supper together as a family), everyone understands that no one eats until the cook is seated. It's called *manners.* And no one leaves the table without asking to be excused. It's called *manners.* And when dessert is served, my kids have been taught to wait until the hostess grants permission before digging in. It's called *manners.* (Our youngest, age 8, recently gave a verbal warning to some adults who broke the latter rule. "Hey," he said while gaining their full attention–"Don't you know you're not supposed to eat cake until she sits down!") Hmm. Kids–they can leave you feeling embarrassed and bursting with pride all at the same time.

I grew up opening the door for ladies (and still do). It's called *manners.* I never called older people by their first names and always said "Yes sir" or "No ma'am" (and still do). It's called *manners.* And I was taught by my parents to look people in the eye, shake a firm hand, and say "thank you" a lot. It's called *manners.*

And may I add a 21st century high-tech addition to the manners equation? When you are attending a movie or a wedding or sitting in a church service–*turn off your stupid cell-phone!* Wow! It felt good to say that!

Simple kindness and basic acts of common courtesy seem like a small thing but then, again, life is made up of small things–like *manners.*

Fighting the Urge to Exercise

Every now and again I get the urge to get into shape. It's nothing I get fanatical about but I do realize that moderate exercise is good for you. One year, I talked my wife into buying me an exercise bike. I had dreams of riding that baby all through the winter months and getting back into shape. I rode it. Hard. Twice. It became an expensive towel rack.

Remember those velour workout suits that were the rage in the '80s? We were into "fashion exercise" back then. If we were going to sweat, at least we would look good doing it. The problem was, by the time you put on those velour outfits, you weren't motivated to work out, you were motivated to take a nap! And remember Richard Simmons? *"Sweatin' to the Oldies..."* You ladies still have that VHS tape in the drawer, don't you? Very strange man.

As one sage said, "Whenever I get the urge to exercise, I lie down until it goes away."

I love walking in the great outdoors. There is something about fresh air and being outside that grabs your senses (and allergies) and makes you come alive. That is, unless the weather is bad or you're under it. Come to think of it, the weather has been bad and I have been under it, so...I haven't been walking much lately.

Someone gave me free tickets to a Tennessee Titans football game. I watched as twenty-two athletes in top physical condition performed on the field in front of 70,000 overweight spectators who were downing hot dogs and pizza and a lot of other stuff that looked hazardous. The people who need exercise cheer on the guys who don't. Go figure.

Speaking of figures... There seem to be three rules in life: (1) "i" before "e" except after "c," (2) if in doubt, don't, and (3) if it tastes good, it's bad. Of course, there are exceptions. For example, Snickers Bars don't count for #3. They are made of chocolate, peanuts, and caramel–good for what ails you *–like hunger!* Do you know how many fat calories are in one candy bar? That's why I eat mine with a diet cola.

And then there are the dreaded "food police." A friend recently had heart trouble, nothing major but a good warning. As a result, his wife makes sure that he eats lots of salads and non-fat, no-fried stuff. And then we go out and get ice-cream. Hey, it's a food group!

The problem is...it's expensive to eat right. Try getting a chicken sandwich off the 99-cent value menu. Not going to happen. Or try feeding a family of four for $10 on anything else but a sack of tacos. Good luck. Sure, all of us could eat better and exercise more. In fact, if you're ready to start, I'll make you a great deal on a mint-condition towel rack with low miles...

Moaning The Doghouse Blues

My wife, bless her heart (there's that southern "blessing" again), loves animals. In fact, I have learned from past experience to accelerate when a stray dog appears alongside a highway. "Did you see that little lost dog? Let's go back and rescue..." I always say the same thing, "What dog?"

When we were married, she had a French Poodle. We didn't get along–at least the dog and I. That dog acted like a cat with an attitude. She says it was because she was old; I said it was because she was from France.

After the French Poodle departed (carefully chosen words), I bought her a little Yorkie Terrier. Do you know how much those dogs cost? Then we had her bred. Do you know how much you can get for Yorkie pups? She had four in all, which we promptly named after Country Music stars–Garth, Dolly, Reba, and Waylon. I wanted to breed her again–maybe get enough money to build a nice deck. My wife said no. Her dog was not that "kind" of dog.

Once she bought a puppy for Luke when he was three. She had this mental image of Lassie and Timmy–you know, little boy growing up with his best friend. She did get him a puppy–a *Great Dane* puppy! The little boy and little puppy idea worked well for three days. After that, he turned into a horse.

She informed me that Great Danes are to be kept indoors. “What?” “Yes, they are short haired dogs and need to live in a climate-controlled environment.” Great. I still remember that dog galloping down the hall and taking over my recliner. “Either he goes or I go!” was my ultimatum. It was quiet for a long time. “What are you doing,” I asked. “I’m thinking it over,” she said.

Once a cow got out when she was eight months pregnant (my wife, not the cow). Who says pregnant women can’t handle cattle? I gained a new sense of respect for her that day.

Then there was the time she wanted goats. We bought two and they were cute—for a week. Goats are like rabbits. Two became four and four became...a headache. I don’t know who originated the phrase, “You get my goat,” but you could sure “get” mine. Free. In fact, we did give them away to a good ol’ boy farmer who showed up in a little pickup to haul them away.

“How you gonna take those goats out of here in that truck?” I asked. “They’ll jump out.”

“Not when I’m finished with ’em,” he said.

And with that, he pulled out a roll of duct tape, flipped over each goat, and proceeded to tie their legs together like a calf roper at the rodeo. It was a beautiful sight.

I don’t know what the future holds but I have a feeling it will always hold a pet or two around our place. And that’s okay—because when my wife reads this column, I’ll be in the doghouse and...I’ll need the company.

Sweet Loretta

There are some people you meet who are extra special. They are handicapped individuals who display no limitations of their disability because no one ever bothered to tell them they were handicapped. My friend, Loretta, was like that. Loretta was mentally handicapped—she had the body of an adult, the mind of a child, and...the heart of God.

I have often wondered why there are people like Loretta. I'm not sure about the answer to that question but I do know that Loretta and others like her give all of us the opportunity to feel a greater sense of compassion and, in so doing, come a little closer to knowing the God she knows.

My wife and I once visited our friend in the hospital. Loretta was having a tough time, had exhibited some aggressive behavior (due to improper medication), and was under observation. They brought her to us in the visitation room. We hugged and sought to make conversation while she remained silent and sipped on some orange juice.

"We just came by to see you and talk for a while," I said.

She stopped sipping, looked at me rather matter of fact and replied quickly, "What do you want to talk about, brother Adams?"

"Uh, well..., I uh, just wanted to talk about...how are you doing?" I asked, awkwardly fumbling for words.

"I am fine," she said, then added, "So what do you want to talk about?"

"Well, I uh, don't know..."

I could see that small talk and chit-chat wasn't going to work well that day for either of us. She wasn't acting herself and the conversation was going no place very fast. So we just hugged her. There are times when you need to stop moving your lips and let your arms do the talking. And that's what we did.

About twenty years ago, Loretta's family took her to Disney World. I had a friend, Chuck Sowers, who worked for the Florida company and when I told him about Loretta and asked if they could give her a little extra attention, Chuck said that he would be delighted to show her some Disney magic. He kept his word and my special friend had a tour to end all tours. She even met the man himself–or at least the "Mouse" himself. It was a dream come true for Loretta and a trip she talked about for years.

I believe people like Loretta add something very valuable to our world–something we may not get any other way. They teach us about love and patience and the value of serving others but, most of all, they teach us about God. I also believe that God has a special place waiting for people like Loretta.

Apparently God decided He couldn't wait any longer and so, a few days ago, He brought Loretta home to be with Him.

Thank you, sweet Loretta, for being my friend. I love you very, very much. And...the next time we're together, something tells me that we'll have a lot to talk about.

Daytona Dads

I finally got it. Whatever has been "going around" this cold and flu season finally found its way to my doorstep. Great. I've got it–and you can have it! Then again, if you are kind enough to read these brief vignettes each week, I consider you a friend. And friends don't wish the flu on friends.

So...I spent Sunday afternoon as a couch potato (does that have an "e" on the end? I'll run it through my Dan Quayle spell checker...) and curled up to watch the Daytona 500. I'm not generally a big fan of NASCAR (although I used to enjoy seeing Petty and Allison and all those good old boys of yester-year) but I do think it is a sport that maximizes the testosterone experience.

My wife says it must be men who are driving because... (1) they go around in circles, (2) they tailgate, (3) and when they do pull in to ask for directions, they don't stay long enough to get it right. I think I even saw a couple instances of road rage. My medicine was beginning to take effect and I was drifting in and out so I'm not sure if it was really Daytona or the traffic channel with live shots from I-65 web cam. Then again, I'm not sure it makes much difference.

I thought of something while watching the likes of Dale Jr., Rusty, and Jeff come roaring into Pit Row. These guys and their team pride themselves on getting in and out of the pit in as little as eighteen seconds. Four new tires, fresh fuel, and whatever else needs attention–in *eighteen* seconds. Who says you can't get good service any more?

The problem is that there are some dad's among us who father like that. They roar home from work like they are coming into Pit Row. They get out, kiss the wife, hug the kids (who are already in bed), grab some supper, watch the news, and hit the sack to get a few hours of sleep before jumping out of bed before dawn (and before the kids are up) to be out the door and back into the race. *Daytona Dads.* Know any?

One study showed that the average American father spends 37 seconds a day with his young children. *Thirty-seven seconds?* Are you kidding? It takes longer than that to brush your teeth! Families whose fathers view their home as a thirty-seven second pit stop are headed for disaster. Wives will sense neglect and kids will be vulnerable–to wrong influences, friends, and behavior. Sure, being a dad is both demanding and daily, but someone will influence your boy and girl. It had better be you.

To a child, love is spelled T•I•M•E. And that's more than a thirty-seven second pit stop. *Daytona Dads*...most of us could do a lot better.

Jingle Bells

They say that *timing* is everything. It's true. For example, the difference between telling a funny joke and a not-so-funny joke is...timing. It also helps to remember the joke. Of course, the older I get the more I find myself starting a story only to rely on my wife to finish it. I guess we're comedians in tandem. It happens at our age.

There are few places where timing is more critical than at a funeral. They say funny things happen at church, but funny things can also happen at solemn occasions like weddings and funerals. I won't go into weddings because usually the funny things have something to do with a bad combination of long-winded preachers and hot-stuffy grooms who faint under pressure. You've seen the videos. I laugh until I cry.

But funerals are different. Funerals are serious (and should be) but even then it is not that unusual for something to go seriously wrong.

Take the preacher I heard about who was "waxing eloquent" (one person misspoke that phrase and repeated it as "waxing an elephant"—I want to see that!) at a funeral service when he became a little too carried away with a metaphoric comparison—comparing the physical body to the shell of a peanut. He said, "What you see in the casket is only the shell of the one we knew. The *nut* has gone home..." Hmm. You're laughing. They did, too.

The one funeral "event" that tops them all occurred in a southern town a few years ago when a man with a beautiful baritone voice was asked by an aged widow to sing a few songs at her dear husband's service. Although he didn't know the departed, he had a wonderful reputation in those parts for performing superbly at such serious occasions.

At the visitation service, he asked the bereaved wife if she had any special requests. After naming a couple of familiar hymns, she said softly, "And there is one more." "Yes," he asked, leaning closer to hear. "Jingle Bells," she said. "Jingle Bells?" he repeated. "Yes, that's the one," she said. "Jingle Bells."

The fellow walked away rather puzzled as he thought about the inappropriateness of singing *Jingle Bells* at a funeral service. As he thought about it further, however, he reasoned that there must have been a purpose behind the rather odd request. Maybe Christmas was a special time for the older couple and perhaps that song brought to them warm memories of family and friends. The more he thought about it, the more he became convinced that he must honor the wishes of the dear departed.

So he did it.

After solo's of familiar and fitting hymns about precious memories and heavenly hope, the fellow paused, cleared his throat and, before a solemn group of hundreds, belted out in his familiar baritone voice—*"Dashing through the snow, in a one-horse open sleigh, o'er the fields we go, laughing all the way, ha! ha! ha!…"* The audience sat stunned and tears began to flow—not tears of loss-of-composure grief but tears that happen when there is loss-of-composure laughter and you get the funnies and can't hold it in.

After the service, the dear widow approached the baritone vocalist and said, "I didn't want *Jingle Bells*… I meant 'Ring Out Those *Golden Bells*.'" *Oops.*

Golden Bells or Jingle Bells? I guess it's all in the timing.

Are We There Yet?

What were we thinking? The last time we loaded up the family in a mini-van and tied down the luggage carrier to the roof rack was in '94 when we made that two-week trip to Colorado. A lot can change in eleven years—like kids grow up and bodies get bigger. So when I spoke recently on a college campus in south Florida, everyone wanted to go. And why not—it's February here and warm there. Besides, who would turn down a free trip to the Sunshine State? *Road trip!!!*

We rented a mini-van. There is a reason they call them "mini" vans...

Years ago I learned that light travels at 186,000 miles per second and if you could somehow travel at that speed, it would take you 4.5 years to reach the nearest star. I can't fathom that. Space travel and galaxies and the speed of light are more than I understand. But here is one irrefutable law of science that I do understand—it is impossible to travel from Nashville to Florida in a crowded mini-van without hearing, "Are we there yet?"—before you get to Murfreesboro. Mark it down.

We survived. We even stayed in a pretty nice place where we had booked adjoining suites—at least they called them suites—more like an extra room with a couch. And with two rooms, I mean, "suites," it meant there were four TV's.

One even worked.

When the maintenance guy finally showed up, he pulled out a little remote control and all the TV's came to life. When I asked if I could have his remote control, he said, "No way, man, this operates all the TV's in the whole hotel." Talk about job security. When I asked why the remote controls in the rooms weren't synchronized with the TV's, he shrugged and said, "I duh-no." And when I inquired how to turn off the TV (since neither the remote nor the buttons on the set itself actually did anything), he shrugged again and said, "Unplug it." Of course when I did, the next morning the set wouldn't come back on. So we called for maintenance and the man with the magic remote. It became routine.

I think I know where they can film the sequel to "Dumb and Dumber."

Funny things are bound to happen when a family of six including two grown kids in their twenties, a sixteen-year-old and a nine-year-old set off for Florida. But we did okay and along the way, we laughed at ourselves–mostly they laughed at me and my driving rules–no fast-food drive-thru (it's quicker to go in), no Interstate crossovers (you must eat and get gas–take that either way–on the same side that you exit), and no stopping at any place that advertises, "See Live Alligators."

It was the ultimate real-life "Survivors." But we made it. And along the miles, we shared some laughs and made some memories. Fact is, give me eleven more years, and I'll be ready to go again. *"Are we there yet?"*

Gladys Dunn

There are more jokes and stories told about preachers than just about anyone else. Lawyers would probably rank up there, too. Then again, I'm especially leery of any joke that begins, "Have you heard the one about the lawyer *and* the preacher?" Bad combination.

Here are a few from my hall of fame collection...

A long-winded visiting preacher was bragging about his ability to create his sermons while driving in the car. "As I drive to distant places to preach, I find that I have hundreds of miles to formulate my thoughts," he boasted. After hearing a particularly long lesson, one fellow shook his hand at the back of the church house and said, "Brother ______, you ever get up a sermon on the way to the corner store? These coast-to-coast sermons are killing us!"

A fellow had heard about all he could stand one evening during a revival meeting and got up to leave. The preacher, feeling rather insulted that this brother would just walk out, stopped his sermon and shouted, "Hey, fella, where do you think you're going?" The man responded firmly, "I'm going to get a haircut!" "A haircut?" the preacher asked. "Why didn't you get one before you came?" "Because," the man hollered back, "when I came, I didn't need one!"

A little girl became restless as the sermon dragged on and on. Finally, she leaned over to her mother and whispered, "Mommy, if we give him the money now, will he let us go?"

Give her an "A" for honesty... A Bible class teacher had her students write Thank You notes to the minister. One little girl wrote, "Dear brother_______, I liked your sermon on Sunday. Especially when it was finished." Carla, age 10.

And then...my #1 favorite of all time...

One preacher I know loves to go overtime—and I mean way overtime. When the service was finally over (sigh) and the congregation had endured another of his famous lengthy orations, one dear sister turned to greet a visitor seated behind her. She introduced herself. "Hello," she said. "I'm Gladys Dunn." The visitor sighed and said, "Whew! I'm glad he's done, too!"

Sometimes it's good to laugh at yourself. You might as well, because if you don't, someone else will.

Tuesday Mornings with Bubba

Ever have a morning when you know it's going to be "one of those days?" It's nothing major or life-changing, just minor annoyances similar to that Lone Ranger mosquito that buzzes your ear when you're trying to sleep on a hot summer night. You know, the mosquito that sounds like a Blackhawk Helicopter hovering just inches above your right ear. Yes, that kind of annoyance.

I had "one of those days" last Tuesday. I'm not sure why it happened on Tuesday as nothing unusual usually happens on Tuesdays. Mondays seem to get all the "bad day" press, certainly not Tuesday. Wednesday is "hump day," Thursday is almost Friday, and Friday is Friday, and Saturday and Sunday are the "weekend." Then there is "Tuesday." Tuesday is the shy stepchild day of the week–you know, the kind that sits quietly in the corner bothering no one and preferring to be left alone. That's Tuesday.

Occasionally, Tuesday can get an attitude.

And so it was...that on Tuesday morning I noticed a problem. I picked up my office phone and–no dial tone. Fortunately, I live nearby and went home to call the company with whom my office has contracted to provide our service. I guess I could have used my cell phone to call but it was home in the drawer where it stays most of the time. My wife says I should carry it with me. I'm not sure why, since my office is only one half mile away from my home. I mean, how many emergencies happen in one half mile? If I broke down, I could walk home by the time I figured out how to use my cell phone. Besides, I don't know the number anyway. I've also noticed that when people carry cell phones in their holster, they go off all the time with those annoying jingles. So when I do carry it, I keep it on "silent." That way I never hear it.

Don't get me started on cell phones.

The phone service folks sent out a repairman. He was a nice fellow I'll call "Bubba." That's probably not his real name but he looked like a "Bubba." So Bubba, with his belt full of tools, went right to work and in a few minutes proudly proclaimed a diagnosis.

"Hey, I think I've found your problem," he hollered from down the hall.

"Great," I said with a sense of relief.

"Yeah," said Bubba, "the problem is (insert drum roll)... you ain't got no dial tone."

"Really???" I asked.

"Yes sir. You gotta have a dial tone for the phone to work."

Bubba was full of helpful information.

"Can you fix it?" seemed like a logical question to ask.

"Oh, no way," said Bubba.

"Bell South owns all the outside equipment. You'll have to call them."

"But how can I call without a dial tone?" I responded.

"Oh yeah," thought Bubba. "Now that is a problem."

It was that kind of morning. Maybe I'll bring my cell phone tomorrow. Wonder if Bubba knows the number...

Coach Gibbs

Joe Gibbs is one of my all-time favorite people. During the 80s, he led the Washington Redskins to three Super Bowl appearances and two championships. I was privileged once to get a ticket to a sold out playoff game against the Bears. A friend was working for Reagan's re-election campaign and when a big-time Republican donor came to town, they offered her a ticket. Smiling, she said, "Young man, I could care less about football but I wouldn't want you to get into trouble so...take my ticket and give it to a friend." He did, I went, and I've been a Republican ever since.

Gibbs eventually left coaching and took his penchant for winning to NASCAR where he has likewise met with success. And now he has come full circle–back to Washington and the sidelines of the NFL.

But there is another story...

In 1986, we took in a troubled teen. Helen was rebellious–and homeless. Once she had even directed her anger at me by "keying" my car up one side and down the other. Finally, her folks had had all they could take. Oddly enough, she called me.

We decided to give her a chance. There would be strict rules–one of which was that she must get a job and earn her stay. And she did. She landed a job as a morning biscuit-maker at a Hardees Restaurant–but that meant she had to be at work at 5 A.M. and with no car... But a deal is a deal and every morning we would leave bright and early (well, at least early).

Oh yes, Helen loved the Washington Redskins.

Shortly after she arrived, I wrote a note to Coach Gibbs and asked for a favor. Would he write this troubled teen and encourage her to get her life back on track. I wondered as I dropped it in the mail if I was wasting my time because, after all, there are few jobs more time-demanding than that of an NFL head coach.

One week later a letter arrived in the mail. The return address read: "Redskin Park."

Coach Gibbs wrote that young lady a personal note and gave her advice you don't usually hear from sports legends. If I may paraphrase...

> I understand your life has been troubled... You are not alone. But if you want to get things straightened out, you will need to read your Bible. I take my Bible with me wherever I go—even on the plane when we're going to an away game. It keeps me focused and it will keep you focused. Read it often...

He shared other encouraging comments about overcoming adversity. It was especially meaningful and I have never forgotten his letter.

Super Bowl rings and championships may get the glory but it's the small acts of kindness that impact lives. Like a simple letter to a troubled teen signed, "Your friend, Coach Gibbs."

The Million-Dollar Box

Kenny Dale is a talented singer/songwriter who lives in San Antonio, Texas. He is also a good friend. One of Kenny's songs that never made it to the charts is one that never fails to "make it" with the hearts of those who hear it. It's a simple little story that is guaranteed to put a smile on the face of every adult who was once a kid. It's called, "The Million-Dollar Box..."

Poor little rich kid livin' down the street,
Got a million dollar toy just for bein' sweet.
But his mom and daddy got mad at him,
'Cause he was playin' with the box that the toy came in.

He's playin' with the box that the toy came in.
La La La La La, let the fun begin.
It really doesn't matter how much you spend,
'Cause the fun's in the box that the toy came in.

His daddy took the box and threw it away,
But I found it in the alley where we all play.
Well the million-dollar toy might belong to him,
But we got the box that the toy came in!

We're playin' with the box that the toy came in,
La La La La La, let the fun begin.
It really doesn't matter how much you spend,
'Cause the fun's in the box that the toy came in.

You're smiling, aren't you?

It's true. Of all the toys you can give a child, none is better than the box in which it came. Give a kid a box and imagination takes control. A box becomes a tunnel from which to escape the bad guys or a fort under the dining room table from which one can fight off intergalactic creatures from an enemy planet. Give a kid an expensive present in a big box and, more times than not, he would rather play with the box.

Does that say something to you? Does it say that maybe we parents put the emphasis on the wrong things? That maybe, just maybe, we get caught up in the crass commercialism of the Christmas season and forget that our children could do *more* with a lot *less*.

Yes, we buy more but give less. While making sure our kids have what we didn't have, they end up not having what we did have. Chances are, we had a dad who worked hard (sometimes two jobs) and a mom who was home for us when we came through the door after school. We had parents who taught us moral values, took us to church, and read bedtime stories that built character into our lives. And we had mothers and fathers who cared enough to say "No" without worrying about our delicate self-esteem. We had *less* in those days but we had *more*. A lot more.

My friend is right. It really doesn't matter how much you spend, " 'cause the fun's in the box that the toy came in." Maybe it's a lesson we need to re-learn.

Billy Boy

Remember that old American folk song about Billy Boy? Maybe you never listened to the lyrics to learn why ole Billy and his girlfriend never married. Here they are again:

"How old is she, Billy Boy, Billy Boy?
How old is she, charming Billy?
Three times six, and four times seven,
Twenty-eight and eleven,
She's a young thing and cannot leave her mother."

I can remember singing that as a kid (yes, I am that old...) but always thought "she's a young thing and cannot leave her mother" meant that she was fifteen or sixteen years old. Wrong. Look at the verse–it tells you exactly how old she was.

"Three times six..." is 18. "Four times seven..." is 28. "Twenty-eight..." tack on twenty-eight more. "And eleven..." Now add that up: 18 + 28 + 28 + 11. *Billy Boy's girlfriend was 85 years old–and still couldn't leave her mother!* (I've always wondered how old her mother was...)

Yes, leaving Mom and Dad behind is difficult for some. How many new brides make the mistake of saying, "My dad always did it this way..." Or how many new grooms have made the serious mistake of commenting on her cooking with these never-to-be-forgotten words: "My mom always fixed it that way..." Ouch! Yes, frying pans do hurt.

Leave Mom and Dad out of the equation. Find out how

your new groom will do it; find out how your new bride will make it. One of the most remarkable discoveries in the world is to taste things a new bride will make. You don't want to miss that. It's what future stories are made of...

As a public speaker, I am often invited into people's homes for a meal. It's not uncommon to be approached on occasion by a young couple with these words: "We're having you over to our house for dinner on Thursday night. We just got married two weeks ago and you are our first company." Great. Can't you just sense my excitement?

I was in such a predicament once. As we began to pass the various dishes, I noticed that quantity seemed in short supply. As I was dipping the peas onto my plate, the new bride said, "I didn't know how many peas to prepare...so I made enough for everyone to have ten." Ten peas??? Okay... I'll put some back. Don't want to overdose on peas...

As a new groom, my dad made the mistake of complaining once because my mother didn't make biscuits as often as he thought she should. Her reply, "Okay, buster, you want biscuits, you're gonna get biscuits." And he did. For breakfast. For lunch. For supper. And the next day. And the next. Lots and lots of biscuits. She made her point and he learned to keep quiet.

I feel sorry for Billy Boy, 'cause he missed out–on the biscuits and the peas and all the other wonderful stories of young couples in love. Something tells me that you may even have a story or two...

Worry Warts

I read the other day that we are the most worried culture that has ever lived. I believe it. But think of the irony. We live in a time when life expectancy has surged to an all-time high. Scientists and physicians are able to cure more diseases than ever before. We have become the most educated populace of all time when it comes to eating and living healthier. That's a fact.

Here's another fact: in spite of all of this, no group of people has ever been more worried about losing their health. We keep buying magazines and reading articles that seek to convince us of how sick we are. It's depressing. Come to think of it, everyone I meet is sick these days—of something.

Journalist Bob Garfield tracked health-related articles in the *Washington Post*, *USA Today*, and the *New York Times* and discovered that, among other things:

· 59 million Americans have heart disease

· 53 million suffer migraines

· 25 million have osteoporosis

· 16 million struggle with obesity

· 3 million have cancer

· 12 million have brain injuries... etc.

Garfield's results are *shocking*. And why? They are shocking because his research found that a total of 543 million Americans are seriously sick. 543 million Americans! Wow! What is especially amazing is that 543 million Americans are seriously sick in a country whose total population is...*266 million!*

Maybe we are sicker than we thought! Not only is *everyone* sick but now everyone is twice as sick. Good grief.

It reminds me of all those worriers who want to save us from everything. Look at our cars. First we had simple seat belts but that wasn't enough. Then we had shoulder belts but...shoulder belts without seat belts did more harm than good, so we built contraptions that put the two together. Now we have air bags—even side air bags. As one writer said, "Pretty soon we'll be riding around in a giant marshmallow."

Obviously, worry sells.

Listen, one of the first things you have to learn about life is this: *everything is risky.* Everything. I read the other day that half a million people require emergency room treatment each year for injuries sustained while falling out of bed. Apparently, even getting up is risky.

Ellen Guder wrote:

"You can live on bland food so as to avoid an ulcer, drink no tea, coffee or other stimulants in the name of health, go to bed early, stay away from night life, avoid all controversial subjects so as to never give offense, spend money only on necessities and save all you can. *And you can still break your neck in the bath tub, and it will serve you right.*"

Yes, there are 543 million sick Americans in a nation of 266 million people. Now I'm really worried.

Why Can't You Be Like Your Brother?

My brother is a very strange man. Then again, he thinks I am strange. But it's always been that way. We don't look or act anything alike—he's shorter, I'm taller, he's balding and I'm receding; he's smart and has put his aeronautical engineering degree at work with the FAA in Washington, D.C., and I'm...well, I'm not him. Listen, when we were in school, my brother had the most boring report cards—A, A, A, A, A, *ad nauseam.* At least mine had variety! Pick a letter. It was there.

Why can't you be like your brother? My parents never said that. Unlike others who play the awful game of parental favoritism, my mother and father loved both sons equally. Both boys, although different in personality and temperament, found love and encouragement in a family environment that nurtured mutual respect among all. I only wish that all children could experience the same, for all children deserve the same.

We have four children and it is amazing that none are "like." Chances are pretty good that the same is repeated in your home today, as it was equally true when you were growing up with your siblings. Even identical twins are not identical, as each child has his/her own peculiar likes and dislikes.

Your children did not come off an assembly line; they were not mass-produced. No two snowflakes alike? That's nothing compared to the fact that no two people are alike.

Doesn't that say something about the unlimited power and creativity of God? Think of all the *billions* of people who have walked on this planet and *each of them* is "one-of-a-kind."

Why can't you be like your brother? Maybe your child cannot answer that question, so I will. They are not "like" because they are not "like." Your child was hand stitched by a God determined to make a child unlike any other. His mind was woven intricately with the finest of neurological threads. Her emotions were given a distinct texture. Their personality was cut from a distinct pattern never to be used again. Amazing!

It's true, isn't it? Some kids are strong and determined while others are easily influenced. Some are creative and dreamy while for others everything is black or white. Some are stubborn and aggressive while others qualify for the Mr. Cooperation and Miss Congeniality awards. Some kids walk around half the day with a dirty diaper and a smile while others are drama kings and queens worthy of a Broadway performance.

Why can't you be like your brother? Quit comparing your children and start understanding them for who they are. I have this theory about why some kids rebel—perhaps they sense that their parents have never really bothered to know *them*. They may be right.

I like my brother but I am not *like* my brother. God made me different and that's okay. Besides, I'm better looking anyway. *Are not. Am, too. Are not. Am, too. Get over on your side and quit touching me! Da-a-a-d...*

Weddings

Getting me to go to a wedding is like getting me to go to the dentist. I'll go only under protest. The way I look at it is simple: I showed up for my own and that ought to be enough. (And all the guys shouted: "A-men!")

My wife recently attended a wedding. I couldn't go, as our son had a ballgame and since someone had to take him, I volunteered. Again, I sacrificed. After the ceremony, there apparently was one of those receiving lines (does anyone really enjoy going through a gauntlet of groomsmen and bridesmaids, feigning conversation?) and when my wife finally made it to the end, the bride gave her a hug and said, "Whew! I'm just glad the hard part is over." "Honey," responded my beloved, "the hard part just started." (And all the gals shouted: "A-men!")

New brides. They are so naïve. Grooms, too. But weren't we all?

I heard a story of a man who fell in love with an opera singer. He could never get close enough to really know what she was like as his view was always through binoculars and from the third balcony. He fell in love with her voice and although she was much older than he, it didn't matter. "With a voice like that," he said, "I could live happily ever after." He set his mind upon one thing–marriage.

After a whirlwind romance and a hurry-up ceremony, off they went on their honeymoon. He watched that first night as she prepared for bed. He watched her pull off her wig, rip loose her false eyelashes, yank out her false teeth, pluck out her glass eye, unstrap her wooden leg, remove her hearing aid... In absolute horror, he shouted, "*For goodness sake woman, sing, sing,sing!*"

Most of us are like that. We get married looking at our future mate through binoculars from the third balcony. It's only after the ceremony that we begin to understand how hard this really is.

Someone has said that marriage is a 50-50 proposition. That's dumb. You give half and she gives half is a recipe for failure. Each had better give 100% if you hope to survive.

I heard the story of a lady who didn't get married until she was thirty-one. She didn't worry about it but she did pray about it. Each night she hung a pair of men's pants on her bedpost and knelt to pray this prayer:

"Father in heaven, hear my prayer,
And grant it if you can;
I've hung a pair of trousers here,
Please fill them with a man."

And God did. Not only did she marry at age thirty-one, in the years that followed they had twelve children. Better be careful for what you pray!

After every wedding there comes a marriage. Carriages turn back into pumpkins and wedding gowns go into hibernation in a box destined for the attic. And then the real work begins. But...it's worth it.

The Magic of Yellowstone

I don't know if it was the crispness of the morning mountain air that took hold of me or if it was the bald eagle soaring against the backdrop of the Yellowstone River, but whatever it was I stood mesmerized in a very magical place. I had come to walk into the wilds of the nation's oldest Park—the granddaddy of them all—*Yellowstone.*

It's hard to describe the vastness of this place. The Winnebagos and tour buses see only a small portion of a park larger than some states. But we came to experience Yellowstone the way it was meant to be experienced—on foot. Up close and personal.

There is something about a trail that disappears into the woods that has always intrigued me. As John Muir writes, "When a man comes to the mountains, he comes home." It's true. My heart comes alive not on a city street or in front of a computer, but in the backwoods where trails can be explored and nature reaches out and grabs the senses.

Maybe that's why I love maps. Give me a map and a trail and I have recaptured the spirit of Peary and Cook, Finn and Sawyer, or Lewis and Clark. I yearn for the road less traveled and for adventure far removed from any prefabricated theme park. I want the real deal, for it is in the wild unknown that a man searches out his soul. After all, Moses did not encounter the living God at the mall but in the wilderness. Maybe that's why Jesus left the population behind and spent so much time there. Wilderness renews the soul.

We took a walk into a topography that has the lilt and roll of heavy seas. We walked into valleys so vast that worries and stress seemed as distant as the snow-capped peaks. We walked under huddles of aspens hung with gold and shimmering in the September sun. We walked past thousands of green spruce and through lodge-pole pines, past canyons and geysers and rivers of glass. We saw waterfalls higher than Niagara, climbed to the 9500' level of Mt. Washburn only to be turned back by strong winds and drifting snow. We saw Shoshone Lake, the largest back-country body of water in the lower 48, and we watched in awe as the remote Lonestar Geyser put on a thirty-minute performance more spectacular than that of Old Faithful.

And wildlife—bears rummaging about for berries, big-horn sheep, elk bugling for companionship, and bison so big and numerous that one wonders if this was how it used to be. This is Yellowstone—a place like none other.

Something tells me that in the days ahead, I will invoke the magic of the land of the yellow stone whenever I need renewed perspective. And when I do, the sprawling wild country will live in my heart all over again.

The Little Store

I remember going with my grandmother to the "little store" (as I called it then) on state line road in Weakley County, Tennessee. It was a small family-run business, a place to buy milk and bread and operated by some pleasant folks who lived next door. I loved to go to the "little store."

I remember the old "Colonial Bread" sign on the wooden screen door and how it made a funny screeching noise as the spring was stretched whenever it opened wide. I recall a dusty checkerboard resting on top of an old barrel in the corner next to the woodstove with a couple of well-worn cane-bottom chairs that had seen plenty of high stakes action over the years. Just across the aisle was an old Coke machine where you could get little 6½ ounces of bottled carbonation. My grandmother always bought one of those and then pried off the cap with a bottle opener tied to a string and left to dangle next to the cash register. But it was the chocolate Yoohoo's that grabbed my attention. A bottle of Yoohoo, a game of checkers, and a few minutes playing with other kids around the "little store" are special memories of a childhood past.

It's easy to forget that America was built on the backs of Mom and Pop entrepreneurs who owned their own business and who worked hard to scratch out a living for their family. From roadside fillin' stations to corner grocery stores, the family-owned-and-operated retail business was the staple of the American economy.

It still is.

Did you know that the vast majority of business in America is small business? Known historically as "Mom and Pop Stores," they employ a greater percentage of the population than all the national franchises put together. But they are in trouble. Government regulations, competition from mega-retailers, and a tendency from the buying public to ignore smaller stores in favor of national franchises, spell trouble for the "little man." And we are losing something precious in the process.

The Mom and Pop stores may not have the name recognition of their big brother national franchises, but they do have *name* recognition—for example, *your name!* Try walking into a mega-retailer and see if they know your name. Fat chance. And, by the way, try being a couple dollars short and see if they will extend you credit on a handshake until the next time you are in. Fatter chance. And the next time you are at a local high school football game, take a look at the advertising banners that line the field or flip through a school yearbook and see who it is that advertises and supports the school programs where your children attend. The people giving are probably those who can least afford it. But they do it anyway.

Think about that the next time you pass a small business. That "little store" just happens to be the staple of your community. *Your* community. And they deserve your support. And...if you are a dollar short, it's okay. They know your name.

Steve

This is about a kid who wasn't supposed to make it, a youngster without the advantages of others. It's a story about a young man who succeeded in life in spite of the hand he was dealt. It's a story that renews faith in America and hope for the young people of tomorrow. It's a true story about...*Steve.*

The fall of 1979 was when I made the decision to get involved. It was one of those NFL ads promoting the Big Brother Program for disadvantaged kids—the one where a football player puts his arm around a needy child and says, "The United Way, it works for all of us"—that got to me. I made the call.

I was quick to learn that there were more kids needing role models and "big brothers" than there were volunteers to help. But I also knew that at least I could make a difference in the life of one.

I chose a young man named Steve.

I'm not sure why. Maybe it was because he seemed so unsure of himself. Maybe it was because he sat alone in the corner while the other boys were loud and boisterous. Maybe it was because he looked like the kid who always got picked on. My heart went out to Steve.

Steve lived with his mother in a small apartment in a tough part of town. She was a good woman trying her best to raise her children in hard times. Steve's dad had deserted the family when he was an infant and, although he later knew his dad, there was never any closeness. Life wasn't easy for Steve but never once did I hear him complain.

Afternoons, weekends, and any spare time was spent with Steve. We wrestled, played catch, raked leaves, went camping, and generally did what dads do with sons. He was there the day our oldest daughter was born. I can still see his little face bursting with pride as he peered over the ledge and into the nursery where Sharon slept.

Time went on and Steve grew into a responsible young man. I lectured to him time and again that in America dreams take you as far as you are willing to go. By the time I drove Steve to college (yes, college!), the quiet, shy little boy of yesterday had grown into a polite young man with an outgoing personality and an unlimited future.

Steve finished college. Today, Steve manages a successful Edward Jones investments firm in Alabama, is married to a wonderful lady, and together they have three great kids. One more thing...Steve and Cindy just returned from China where they adopted a beautiful little girl who had been abandoned at an orphanage. Somehow I always knew that Steve would "play it forward"—invest his life into someone else who needed him.

You *can* dream big in America. You *can* work hard and make those dreams come true. Just ask Steve...

Raising Daughters

Done. I put the paintbrush down and looked over my work with a tinge of satisfaction. It wasn't easy, but I did it and I was finished. We had just moved our teenage daughter downstairs to a room that was more private and spacious than the one across the hall from us. It has become a rite of household passage as she now occupies the same room held previously by her older sister. It's just that...well, it looks different now. It's pink and black.

My friend, Mike, laughed at me when I picked up the paint at his store. "What colors?" he asked. "Pink and black" was my hand-over-the-mouth-don't-say-it-too-loud response. "Pink and black?" he repeated, as if he had somehow misunderstood. Then with a grin, he asked, "Teenage daughter?" How did he know? He knows because he has one. And she has a green room. Not a soothing kind of forest green but a reach-out-and-grab-you green. Her dad painted it for her. Her dad will repaint it after she moves out. It's a "dad" thing.

Teenage daughters.

I have long been an advocate of saying "Yes!" when you can say yes because the "No's! will certainly be in the majority when raising teenagers. I have also learned that the path to peace is paved with overlooking some things—like rooms that should be featured on the Weather Channel's Storm Stories—perfectly good clothes and personal items scattered about with reckless abandon. For the life of me, I do not understand that. I live by the motto of the Naval Academy—"Everything has a place, and a place for everything." My kids think I'm weird.

Sometimes I just shut the door. It's easier that way.

I've raised both teenage boys and teenage girls and the girls give you a better run for the money. At least on some things. Teenage males are into testosterone, which means wrestling, football, and any competitive game. A teenage boy I understand because I've been there/done that. Teenage girls, on the other hand, perplex me. I don't always know what they are thinking because they don't always know what they are thinking. They talk on the phone a lot, and get excited about stuff that well...doesn't seem all that excitable. And they want their rooms painted funny colors.

They take long showers, too. "I have to take long showers because I have to shave my legs," is her explanation. Come to think of it, my son took long showers and he didn't have to shave his legs. It's a "teen" thing.

"This, too, shall pass." My wife says that all the time. She's right. But in the meantime raising teenagers will try your patience and test your will. I find myself smiling sometimes at younger parents who live in a neat little black and white world while promising the rest of us that... "I'll never let my teenager..."

Not everything is black and white. Sometimes you have to add a little pink.

Break a Vase

Sometimes it's okay to splurge. Remember the story in the Bible about the woman who anointed Jesus with some very expensive perfume? A few small-minded people criticized her for such an act of extravagance. Jesus didn't. In fact, He praised her for the gift. She had splurged. Sometimes it's okay to splurge.

My wife was cleaning cabinets the other day and brought out her collection of vases. Mind you, there is nothing special about the vases except that each vase represents a time when I brought her flowers. I wasn't smart enough to buy just the flowers and bring them home and re-use an old vase—I just bought a new vase. The flowers are long gone, but the vase collection remains. They make her smile.

Break a vase.

It's a saying around our house for when we do something entirely off-the-wall and unexpected. Something extravagant. Something extra. Something un-Dave Ramsey. You don't break a vase every day or every month but once in a while it's okay to go first class—a dinner out at an expensive restaurant, an overnight at a fancy hotel, a visit to the jewelry store.

And sometimes it doesn't cost a thing.

A few years ago when my wife was working part-time at Baptist Hospital, she would arrive home about midnight. It was one of those crazy weeks when we hadn't seen each other very much and needed to have a creative "date." It was also one of those weeks when we didn't have any money. So I broke a cheap vase.

She came home at the stroke of twelve to find a candlelit table waiting. I put out the good stuff—tablecloth, china, silver, sparkling grape juice in those fancy goblets—whatever I could find that looked expensive. And I dressed up—put on the best suit I had. Listen, I wasn't taking my lady out to some greasy spoon dive. No way. This was to be a night I wanted her to remember.

She was escorted to her seat (by the window!) and served the finest cuisine I have ever learned to prepare. Toast. Not cheap white bread but wheat. And served with wonderful blackberry jelly. And butter (the *real* deal). We dined on fine china and drank from those fancy goblets and talked...and laughed...and cried. At least she cried. I don't know if she cried because it was unexpected or because I had burnt the toast...but we had fun.

Sometimes you don't have to spend any money to break a vase.

Got a little boy? Take him fishing. Got a little girl? Take her on a "leaf walk" and make a memory. Got a parent still around? Sit down and talk. Got a spouse? Do something a little extra—a card sent to his work, fresh flowers for her, burnt toast by candlelight.

Life's too short. Break a vase.

A Just Cause

The following came to me from a forty-something friend who is currently serving his country in Baghdad, Iraq. My friend makes me very proud.

> There is an old saying that no one prays for peace like a soldier. I never truly appreciated that until 9-11. Since Vietnam, the U.S. has gone in, done the job, and got out with little bloodshed or stayed for peace-keeping operations that have been long but quiet. Now, while small considering the history of war, the price is high. Soldiers, innocents, and the misguided are dying. Why? Simple.
>
> Evil.
>
> There is no doubt that these Muslim extremists are evil personified. While I hate to be here, here is where the evil is. President Bush has stated many times that he would prefer to fight them abroad rather than at home. I could not agree more. I want nothing more than to be home with my family but as corny as it may sound, someone has to do this.
>
> I do not believe that any rational argument can be made against our country's action. There are critics sitting in their imagined safety maligning a leader who bears the responsibility of every life put in harm's way. How can these shortsighted "patriots" undermine the efforts of our country? When the war is over, they can, and should, examine all they want.

For now, they should understand that assigning personal motive, careless disregard for life, and even lies about our government help the terrorists.

I am here. I don't just see it—I live it. The president is not responsible in some sort of malicious way for the deaths and injuries. But his opponents, blinded by ambition, are becoming a focal point of anger among the soldiers. They think they are supporting us. They will *never* understand that they are not.

We all have seen what these terrorists are capable of in the name of their god. I pray for my enemy. I pray that they will find a way other than violence. I pray that they will find God. I pray that they will see the death of a human being as more tragic than that of a dog. Until those prayers are answered, I pray for the success of our country. I pray that a nation founded on belief in God will turn to Him. I pray for the safety of each soldier walking the Iraqi streets. I pray that evil will be defeated.

If I have stepped on any political toes, it was not meant to be mean-spirited. It is simply the way we see it over here. We vent to one another, but we are sitting in the proverbial choir. I could go on and on but I won't. Please pray for us.

Sign me,

A Christian and an American Soldier from
Robertson County, Tennessee

Love Is...

I talk occasionally to some youth groups about relationships, love, and dating. (A couple years ago I attended an invitation only "dating conference" held at the Nashville airport Marriott and taught by Dr. John Morris, a famous scientist, geologist, and author. Dr. Morris spoke on the subject of "dating"—i.e., dating *rocks*. It wasn't especially exciting but...they did feed me a free breakfast, so it was okay.)

As I listened to Dr. Morris, I got to thinking about... how "love" must be hard for the evolutionist (since he believes people are the mere by-product of chance). Somehow I imagined the evolutionist sitting on a front porch swing, looking at the moon and trying to win the heart and hand of his girl with these romantic words, "You know, the molecules of my brain have arranged themselves in such a way that I have kindly feelings toward you..." Oh boy! Isn't that exciting???

Listen, the three magical words in any language are: *"I love you."* And do you know why they are special? Because God is and because God made man in His image and gave man the capacity to love. As the song suggests, "Love is a wonderful thing"–it's a wonderful thing because it is a God-thing.

Love. We throw that word around so much that it has lost its meaning. Ask teenagers to define "love" and they typically use the word *feelings*–as in *"Oh, What a Feeling!"* (By the way, if that is your definition of "love," then go get a Toyota–that's their slogan!) Love is not about feelings because...even though feelings are a good thing, feelings fluctuate. *Love is deeper.* And romance is good but romance is tied to feelings. *Love is deeper.*

Love is...*commitment.* It is not feelings that cause a couple to celebrate a 50th wedding anniversary. It is *commitment*: ...for better or for worse. ...in sickness and health. ... in good times and bad. That is what L•O•V•E is all about. (Yes, I know...it's also about picking up his socks off the floor–again! or... reaching blindly for a towel only to find yourself wiping your face with a pair of her pantyhose–it's that stuff, too). The bottom line: *Love is*...keeping your promise and staying committed. Regardless.

Commitment. We need more of it.

Summer

"In the good ol' summertime..." There *is* something good about summer. Really good. The fact is, the warmer months just happen to be my favorite season of the year (at least until Fall!). Maybe it's because I have so many nostalgic recollections about June, July, and August. Maybe it's because warm weather and bright sunshine brings out the best in people. Maybe it's because there are special sights and smells that are exclusively "summer."

Is there a smell in all the world like fresh-cut grass? That's summer. Or the feel of clean cotton? That's summer. Or when a little-leaguer sees a big-league baseball field for the first time. That's summer. You can't beat summer. No way.

Summer is...BLT's with homegrown tomatoes, sweet

corn, and flagging down the ice-cream man in the silly looking truck with the little jingle that gets stuck in your head for days.

It is...going barefoot, catching lightning bugs with your grandchildren, and watching the world go by from your front porch.

It is also...distant thunder, spitting watermelon seeds, Independence Day, family reunions, sunsets, sunflowers, vacations ("Are we there yet?"), theme parks, National Parks, picking blackberries, drive-ins, gardens, clotheslines, car shows, playing catch, back yard burgers, croaking bull frogs, bumblebees, outdoor weddings, convertibles, putt-putt golf, boat rides, short sleeves, sunscreen, camping out, fireworks, popsicles, funeral home fans, fresh cut roses, squirt guns, kiddie pools, long days and dog days.

Summer is all of that–and more! It's flip-flops and fishing poles, picnic tables and shade trees, summer camp and football two-a-days, root beer floats and farmer tans, lemonade stands and lawn sprinklers, shelling beans and shucking corn, pitching horseshoes, wearing no shoes, Vacation Bible schools, and no school.

Summer. I know we complain about the weather in the summer–"H.H.H."–hazy, hot, and humid. But that's probably because we have to balance out the complaining we did in the winter–"C.C.C."–cloudy, cold, and crummy.

Summer. I love it because...I get to feel like a kid again.

Good Stuff

The Good Book says in Ecclesiastes 11:7, "The light is pleasant and it is good for the eyes to see the sun." That is picturesque speech and poignant ancient poetry, coupled with a tinge of rhythmic beauty. Say what? Okay. Here it is in plain talk: God means for you to walk outside, look up at the sun, and *enjoy* life. ***Question***: Are you alive? (Okay, dumb question...) Then thank Him for another day to imbibe of His bountiful goodness and go drink deeply from the well of His blessings. In other words, *quit complaining and seize the day!*

I believe that we dwell too much on all the cloudy, dark, and negative stuff. And there is plenty of that to go around. We go to bed at night watching newscasts with stories of rape, kidnapping, gang violence, child molestation, wife battering, drug busts, bank robberies, terrorism, steroid-using athletes—the list seems endless. Then, to top it off, we grab the morning paper and get yet another heavy dose of "bad stuff" to start the next day. (No wonder we are paranoid!)

Know what I think? I think...we forget that there are a lot of bright and sunny things, too. Like what? Like...

A toddler who falls asleep on the couch in his dad's arms. The Special Olympics. Silver Queen corn and blackberry cobbler. A five-pound bass. A game of Rook with friends. A bright red sunset. A Tennessee orange moon. Sweet tea. A comfortable old sweatshirt. That first spring hamburger on the grill. Red barns. Old trucks. Miniature golf. Andy Griffith re-runs. Morning coffee. Little league baseball. Banana pudding. Old Glory. A song that turns back time. Red Corvettes. Well-worn blue jeans. Girl Scout thin-mint cookies. A good book. Grandparents. Golden Retrievers. A walk on the Greenway. Pizza. A longer walk on the Greenway. Smoothies. Listening to oldies. School papers on the 'fridge. The Smoky Mountains. The smell of fresh-cut grass. Candles. Picture albums. Hugs from kids who are never too old. Horses. Birthdays. The Tooth Fairy. A birdie on a tough hole. The zoo. America. County fairs. Front porches...

Make your own list. We are experts at counting problems and cataloging complaints. Sure, we live in the real world and there are problems, but not everything is awful. So skip the bad news for once and try looking on the *bright* side. There is a whole lot of...*good stuff.*

Thou Shalt Not Steal

Remember the *Ten Commandments*? You know, the ones causing so much controversy these days... Do you recall how they were originally etched in stone? Perhaps God cut them into the rock so that we wouldn't forget them. And for good reason, as man has always displayed a tendency to bend the rules.

Commandment #8 prohibits stealing. It is straightforward and to the point: *You shall not steal.* Got it? Don't steal; don't take what is not rightfully yours.

Thievery is everywhere and, as a result, we are paranoid about it. As if locks on our cars and houses were not enough, we now back up everything with alarms. Of course, they malfunction a lot and most of us don't pay much attention to them. Come to think of it, we have one of those fancy systems for our home. It is supposed to stop intruders. Does it work? I don't know. I think our dog would probably be a better deterrent. (Just put out an A.P.B. for a grungy looking guy with lick marks all over his body.)

It reminds me of a sign someone saw in a front lawn. It read: "Property Protected by a Pit Bull with *AIDS!*" I think that would work.

Sometimes, however, it seems to me that we have soothed our collective consciences by reducing #8 to reading: "Don't steal anything BIG..." Let's see, that should cover looting, grand theft auto, and bank robbery. I don't know about you, but I'm feeling pretty good about #8. Put a check mark by that one.

Not so fast. Have you ever...

- taken a towel from a motel room?
- taken extra change from a clerk who made a mistake?
- taken undeserved deductions on your income tax?
- taken home extra supplies from your job?
- taken answers from someone else's test?

See a pattern? I think the key word is *taken*—as in: *taking* what doesn't belong to you. The world is filled with takers. I have a simple theory that it all starts in grade school with that "innocent" little rhyme: "Losers weepers; finders keepers." Hmm. Is that what we really want to communicate to our kids?

I believe we are often tested not by the BIG stuff but by our honesty in little things.

Makes you think, doesn't it?

Whatever Happened to Summer?

I always thought summer was what happened between Memorial Day and Labor Day. According to the calendar, summer begins on June 21 and ends on September 22—but who goes by that? Every American knows that "summer" falls between those two great Monday shopping days. Or at least it used to.

Aren't kids supposed to be out of school for the summer? Isn't it written in the Declaration of Independence that everyone is created equal and that school vacation commences the end of May and resumes on the Tuesday that falls after the first Monday in September? And doesn't it say that you are endowed by the Creator with three full months of driving your parents crazy with the daily whine—"But, Mom, there's nothing to do..."

I had a friend who goofed off one year and had to go to summer school. Now, everyone goes to "summer" school. It's called *August*.

So here I am, looking at the calendar and realizing that my kids go back to school next week. *Next week???* It's back to fighting morning traffic, buying school supplies, and doing homework. Yes, homework! My daughter informs me that her English teacher has assigned *me* homework—several pages for *me* to read, sign, and file. Uh. Excuse me; *she* is the one in school...

And let's talk about school supplies. We tell our kids that money doesn't grow on trees and then send them off to school where teachers think it must: stapler, hole puncher, whiteout, pens, pencils, pencil sharpener, paper, folders, notebooks, small assignment notebooks, trapper keepers, backpacks, *ad nauseam* (a Latin term meaning—*It's only the first of August, for crying out loud!*). Whatever happened to a pen, a #2 pencil, and a notebook of paper separated by those yellow dividers? Now that was simple.

Did I mention backpacks? Have you ever tried to lift a school backpack lately? (I have this theory on the increase in adult hernia operations, but I won't go into that.)

And get ready for the fees. As in M•O•N•E•Y. I never have any money during the school year because my kids wipe me out each morning. It's not the lunch money as much as it is all the other stuff they forget to tell me until the last minute. "Hey Dad, I need $5 for the book fair, $10 for the science fee, and $20 for the field trip." Great.

I haven't even mentioned new clothes. I saw a sign the other day that read, "Only ___ more shopping days until... school." It's the same sign they put out the first of October for...*Christmas.*

School. It's not so bad, I guess. At least this year I'm ready. I'm taking out a home equity loan to cover the supplies and I've bought a pickup truck to haul the backpack. It's almost August. Bring it on.

This and That

I read the other day that our national weight is increasing. I didn't realize they weighed nations but I suppose the good ol' USA *has* been tipping the scales a bit on the heavy side. I also heard that the airlines might have to raise prices due to a recent increase in "passenger load" (I think I've sat beside a few folks with increased "passenger load"). Sure, doctors tell us to exercise more and watch our diet. But that's hard to do when fast-food is so tempting and we are prone as a people toward more and more busyness. I used to ride an exercise bike. I rode it religiously–for about a week. It became a very expensive towel hanger. So much for exercise.

Speaking of the need for exercise...one of my favorite summer things is to visit Thomas Drugs in the quaint little village of Cross Plains, Tennessee, for a hand dipped ice-cream cone. There is something nostalgic about sitting at the old-fashioned soda fountain while perusing their unique gifts and collectibles. Okay, it may add a pound or two, but you'll feel ten years younger!

There is one in every town... From Maine to Minnesota, there will be one traffic light in town that seems to malfunction regularly–and turn green for everyone but me. It's a conspiracy, right? It's always nice to sit and watch as others get a chance to move on in life while you are stuck in some kind of traffic light time warp. Maybe it's God's way of teaching me patience. He must think I need a lot of lessons.

Crazy and spontaneous... A few years ago we were short on cash and needing a get-away so we did one of the craziest things ever. We packed an overnight bag, jumped in the car and drove...two miles to one of the local motels over by the Interstate. The kids played in the pool and then later we popped some corn and watched a movie. We could have been in Bismarck, North Dakota for all we cared. I even went home long enough to check on the horses and feed the dog. The next morning we ate a free breakfast, packed up the car, and drove all the way home and not one time did the kids yell, "Are we there, yet?"

That's my story and I'm stickin' to it... Our state just passed a new car-seat law that mandates that children up to age nine must be in a car-seat. You're kidding, right? Listen, when my son was eight years old, he was nearly five feet tall and weighed 110 pounds. "Okay, boy, get into your car seat..." That's a good one. By the way, don't you think it's a bit hypocritical when legislators put the emphasis on car-seat safety and look the other way when it comes to alcohol-related issues? If the car-seat legislators are really concerned about public safety, they need to start revoking beer licenses from eating establishments. Or perhaps enforce a sobriety checkpoint on the way out of the restaurant. Ridiculous, you say? Not any more than getting a 110 pound eight-year-old into a car seat. Lots of luck.

The Weather

Have you given attention as to how much the *weather* dominates our lives? It's difficult for people to meet and engage in casual conversation without one or the other bringing up the weather.*"Sure has been hot and muggy lately,"* someone says (which always makes me wonder if they were expecting something different in July).

But one weather-phrase I hear seems to be more national than regional.*"If you don't like the weather here, just wait about thirty minutes and it'll change."* I've heard people in Denver, Colorado say that. And Bangor, Maine. And Chicago. Ditto for Washington D.C., Houston and Pittsburgh.

Interesting thing about the weather–it changes and then it doesn't. While the weather may change from day to day, in the bigger picture of things, weather patterns remain pretty much the same. It doesn't snow here in July. Hurricanes form in the fall, not spring. And when was the last time you heard someone complain about the "dog days of April?"

Sometimes people ask me what I would do if I weren't doing what I am doing. That's an interesting question and the answer is: I would be a meteorologist. But I'll be the first to admit that a little weather goes a long way. Ask my kids. They tend to roll their eyes when dad begins to expound about barometric pressure, low pressure systems, and dew points. *"Uh, oh. Here he goes again..."*

I did stay with a Virginia family once whom I felt were extreme about the weather. Tired of all the sex-coms on television, they opted instead to watch only the weather channel. They popped corn, offered soft drinks and we sat around for three evenings and learned about tornados, blizzards and hurricanes. I'll be the first to admit that it was a little much, although it was clean and there wasn't any bad language.

I recently had an exciting story to tell my family after returning from a trip to Dallas. *"Guess what celebrity I sat behind on the trip down?"* I asked. They started naming off pro football players, movie stars, and music personalities. "Nope," I said. "Are you ready for this? Hold on to your seats, but I flew with *Lisa Patton!"* "Who?" they asked with a quizzical look. "Lisa Patton"–you know, she does the local weather on channel 2." *"Oh,"* they said with a tinge of disappointment. (Okay. Flying with a local weather personality may not rank as high as hanging out with a football player or country music star, but for a weather-wannabe, it was pretty exciting).

And for those of you whose travels take you through the mid-state of Tennessee–let me throw you a little weather advice: *If you don't like the weather around these parts, that's okay. Fact is, just wait about thirty minutes and it'll change.*

Passionate About The Passion

It's about time.

It's about time...that a film is released that is different from the normal barrage of sex-and-debauchery that has become the standard. For years, we have been told that Hollywood only produces what the public wants to see while denying any market value for stories upholding moral and biblical values. *The Passion of the Christ* proves them wrong.

It's about time...that the story of Jesus Christ is told from the viewpoint of history. Previous films about Christ have bordered on the blasphemous–*The Last Temptation of Christ*, or *Jesus Christ, Superstar* to name just two. Jesus was a real person and the historical narratives of four men (Matthew, Mark, Luke, and John) tell His story. They are historians of the highest order and their story is the greatest ever told.

It's about time...that Christians find an expression in the media that upholds their faith. We have tolerance and free expression in this country for every cause but one–Christianity. The Culture of Far Left America has made a mockery of marriage, produced filth masquerading as entertainment, and reshaped our laws so that we bow before the god of political correctness. And I'm sick of it.

It's about time...we understand that the issue is not what specific race of people killed Jesus—but that the race of mankind put Him on the cross. The fact that Jesus died willingly is at the heart of the greatest story ever told—and it is a story that Christians (free speech, anyone?) have a right to tell. And must tell.

It's about time...that we understand that Jesus was not "just a good moral man" and all around nice guy. We are so conditioned to see a safe and sanitized Jesus that we forget—we forget that it wasn't His goodness and niceness that caused such turmoil in the first century (or the 21st century!). Jesus claimed to be the Son of God, the Savior of the world. That claim (and the force of evidence behind that claim) will forever make Him the centerpiece of human history.

It's about time...something happens that moves us beyond our penchant for shallow entertainment and makes us look deep within ourselves. This movie is a gut-check. It will hit you hard and shake you to the core. The words on the page of Scripture take on a realness that you will not soon (if ever!) forget. The film ends and you will not move. The only thing you will hear is sobbing.

It's about time...

Thanks, Mom!

Mother's Day may only come once a year on the calendar but every mom reading this knows that *every day* is Mother's Day—mother's day to *clean*, mother's day to *cook*, mother's day to *comfort*, to *correct*, to *carpool*—and every other busy "c" word. Thus, Mom, in honor of you and...to make sure you know you are remembered each day, I give you the following anonymous observations from innocent children about their mothers. I hope it puts a smile on your face.

- ***Why did God make mothers?***
  Because she's the only one who knows where the Scotch tape is.
- ***How did God make mothers?***
  He used magic plus some super powers and lots and lots of stirring.
- ***What ingredients are mothers made of?***
  God makes mothers out of clouds and angel-hair and everything nice in the world and then He adds one dab of mean.

- ***What kind of little girl was your mother?***
  I don't know because I wasn't there, but my guess would be that she was bossy.
- ***What did your mom need to know about your dad before she married him?***
  She had to know if he was a crook or something. And does he drink beer. And does he make $800 a year. And does he say *no* to drugs and *yes* to chores.
- ***Why did your mom marry your dad?***
  My grandma says that my mom didn't have on her thinking cap.
- ***What is the difference between moms and dads?***
  Moms work at work and work at home. Dads just work at work.
- ***What does your mom do in her spare time?***
  My mom doesn't do spare time.
- ***What would it take to make your mom perfect?***
  On the inside she is already perfect. Outside... maybe some plastic surgery or something.
- ***If you could change one thing about your mother, what would it be?***
  I would make her smarter. Then she would know it was my sister who did it and not me.

Motherhood. May God bless all who venture into this holiest of callings.

Tennessee—The First Time

I've often wondered what it would be like to gaze upon the rolling hills and picturesque farmlands of middle Tennessee for the very first time? Sometimes I think we locals fail to see the beauty around us simply because familiarity breeds—not contempt—but more an attitude of a take-it-for-granted complacency.

That came home to me recently when some Arizona friends came for a visit. We had toured their home state the year before and marveled at the inspiring vistas of the desert landscape. The great Sonora desert dotted by giant saguaro cactus reaching heights of thirty and forty feet is somewhat intimidating to a native of the east. Keeping a sharp lookout for rattlesnakes and scorpions can be a bit unnerving as well. And then there is the heat. Yes, I know... "It's a dry heat"—but so is my oven.

There is something enchanting and charming about the Southwest. The topography stands in sharp contrast to anything we know. There is a sense of ruggedness and adventure that continues to capture the imagination of newcomers. Dust storms, distant thunder, and desert sunsets are nothing short of awe-inspiring.

But not everything is different. Arizona Mills on the south side of Phoenix looks strikingly similar to Nashville's Opry Mills. And the Tucson Cracker Barrel on I-10 sells the same Robertson County, Tennessee rocking chairs and serves up the same down home cooking as does our local counterpart. I mean, who wants authentic Tex-Mex when you can get biscuits and saw-mill gravy?

I wondered about our friends' first-time impressions when they visited here. What would they see that we had missed? Would they be as wide-eyed over Tennessee as we were with Arizona? It didn't take long to find out.

"It's really lumpy here," she said on the ride home from the airport. "Lumpy?" I asked. I looked at my wife and grinned—"Around here we call those *hills*. Lumpy is usually reserved for mashed potatoes." We drove on until she exclaimed with wonder, "How do you people see where you are going? There are trees everywhere!" Yes, the Tennessee landscape stands in sharp contrast to the vast vistas of the Southwest where you can see for miles in all directions.

"What do you think of Tennessee?" I asked John, a sixteen-year-old Tucson native, as we stood in the yard late in the afternoon and looked out toward the barn. He paused for a moment and then said, "I've never seen so much green grass." It's true. In his neck of the woods, well, come to think of it there aren't any woods. Or grass. Grass doesn't grow well in arid Arizona. The fact is: John and his brothers have never known the pleasure (?) of cutting grass. Never.

As we took an evening walk down our little country lane, next to a farm and alongside a creek, she paused and said, "It's just so pretty here." Yes it is. For one week and through the eyes of our western friends, I saw afresh the simple beauty of this place we call home.

Supper with the President

President Bush came to Nashville a few weeks ago for a fundraising dinner costing $10,000 per plate. My wife and I probably would have gone had it not been way over on Hillsboro Road—the other side of town. I mean, with the price of gas these days, who can afford to go that far?

Then again, what kind of country cookin' is worth a combined twenty grand? You know, if those Washington insiders wanted to raise some serious money, maybe they should offer one of those "Buy One Meal, Get the Second for Half Price" incentives. After all, we Southerners will spend anything as long as we have a coupon!

By the way, what kind of tip do you leave when the bill is $20,000? My little water-soaked, wallet-sized "tip card" doesn't go that high.

And did it include dessert? I would hope so.

All of this got me to thinking... I have always wondered what it would be like if the White House (the other White House) would call and say, "Mr. Adams, the President and

First Lady would like to come to your home next Friday night for dinner." First, I would have to remind them of proper protocol—evening meals at our place aren't called "dinner" (only the Sunday noon meal gets that designation), but "supper." And second, come hungry.

Something tells me that Mr. and Mrs. Bush would enjoy eating at our place. Fact is, we would probably go all out and eat out. Outside. On the deck. Fire up the grill—maybe put on some Tennessee pork chops with some Jack Daniels BBQ sauce. And my wife's world-famous baked beans. (Come to think of it, I think she uses "Bush's" baked beans anyway). And iced-tea. Sweetened. And sliced tomatoes. And corn on the cob. And butter. The real deal.

And peach cobbler—with French vanilla decaf coffee. Then again, maybe not. I heard Bush isn't too keen on anything French these days.

"Hey, Mr. President," I say with corn stuck between my teeth and with butter dripping off my chin, "I bet you don't eat like this in Washington!"

Poor guy. I have often wondered how boring it must be with all those stuffy state dinners and foreign dignitaries and food you can't even pronounce. Don't you know... there must be nights when he wishes he could sneak away from the White House and run out and get a pizza like the rest of us?

Yes, we would love to have the President over for dinner. Uh...I mean, supper.

#68 Seth McKinney

I didn't realize how *big* he was until he stood up. We had been sitting across the aisle from each other during a Bible study on a college campus in Tampa, Florida. I noticed him listening carefully to the speaker all the while making multiple notations in his Bible. As soon as the speaker finished, I crossed the aisle and introduced myself.

Now I must tell you that I am not little (6-4, 200 lbs). But Seth McKinney, who is the starting center on the offensive line for the Miami Dolphins would make two of me. Seth, or perhaps I should say, "Mr. McKinney," while equaling my height, is officially listed in the Dolphin media guide at a man-size 305 pounds. We shook hands, engaged in pleasant conversation, and then I introduced him to my son, Luke, a 125-pound, nine-year-old lineman on our local junior pro football team. After all, I figured a couple of tough football guys would have a lot in common.

I talked to Seth about his faith and how it must be difficult being a Christian in the NFL environment. He admitted as much but reminded me that it isn't easy standing upon your convictions in any work environment. "Most guys go to work every day surrounded by people who don't care about the same things you do," he said. He's right. He added, "The toughest part of my job, however, is going on the road. There is one other player with whom I might spend some time but, other than that, I keep pretty much to myself."

I found out later that when he is back in Miami, Seth teaches a teenage Bible class and is very active in his home church in Hollywood, Florida.

Seth McKinney is refreshing to me. A storied football career—a four-year starter with Texas A&M (only the fifth center in NCAA history to start in every game of his college career...), all-Big-12-Conference selection, all-Academic-Big-12 choice, and the number one draft choice of the Dolphins in 2002... On a recent Sunday night game versus the Cleveland Browns, ESPN commentator and former Washington Redskin All-Pro Joe Theisman watched McKinney throw a lead block on an end-around play that gained big yardage and said, "Wow, McKinney looks like a wild buffalo running across the pasture..." I have no doubt that an unknown Cleveland defender would agree with that assessment.

But beyond the accolades that have come his way as a result of his football career, Seth McKinney has his priorities exactly where they need to be. He is a humble man with a heart for God and...has the potential to influence and help a lot of young people.

My son has traded autographed pictures with Seth McKinney. And this year when little league football rolled around, our Luke wanted a new number. He claimed #68—a tribute to his new friend.

You don't hear enough about the "good guys" in sports. It's nice to know that they are still there. Thanks, Seth...I mean, Mr. McKinney.

Remembering Ronald Reagan

There was a brisk wind blowing that spring morning when I stood a few feet from the wingtip of Air Force One at Andrews AFB just outside of Washington, D.C. My mother was in for a visit and she was hoping to see the President. A call came from a friend at the air base saying Reagan was flying out the next day and to be there at 9:00 A.M. We were.

It was the first time I had seen him in person. I remember watching as he descended the steps of Marine One, the famous big green helicopter that ferries Presidents from the White House to local destinations like Andrews or Camp David. I remember that everyone else was bundled up in the cold March wind—everyone except the President. He seemed to be invigorated by the briskness of the morning. Surrounded by an entourage of associates, Reagan walked with an unmistakable ease to the giant 707. He smiled and waved at us—showing an obvious appreciation for ordinary citizens who had come to see him off. I waved back. I remember the chill bumps and the thrill of the moment.

Ronald Wilson Reagan (I don't know why he didn't use his middle name!) was "the Great Communicator." Following the malaise of the 70s, Reagan communicated a message that made patriotism fashionable. His passionate plea at the Berlin Wall to the Soviet Premier—"Mr. Gorbachev, tear down this wall!"—will be remembered forever as the speech that tore away the iron curtain of communism in Eastern Europe. Ronald Reagan won the cold war and brought a newfound freedom to previously impoverished peoples. During his two terms, the small-town boy from Illinois fell in love with the Lee Greenwood song, "I'm proud to be an American," and it became a second anthem during his eight-year presidency.

I saw him on two other occasions while living in Washington—once hearing him give a rousing speech on the two hundredth anniversary of the signing of the Constitution. He was in rare form that day and spoke with passionate energy, combining both wisdom and humor that was typical Reagan.

Ronald Reagan made me proud to be an American. He had a deep-seated faith, an infectious jovial disposition, and a sincere kindness that healed a hurting nation. I conclude with his final public words—a letter written to the American people on Nov.5, 1994 in which he disclosed his battle with Alzheimer's...

> "...let me thank you, the American people, for giving me the great honor of allowing me to serve as your President. When the Lord calls me home, whenever that may be, I will leave with the greatest love for this country of ours and eternal optimism for its future. ...I know that for America there will always be a bright dawn ahead. Thank you, my friends. May God always bless you."

Quiet Time — What's That?

There was something I noticed about all four of our children when they were small. Although possessed (we thought they were all possessed at one time or another!) with unique personalities, they each had one thing in common: they were never tired. Their eyes would glaze over, their speech would slur, their legs would wobble, but if I ever said, "Are you tired?" the answer was *always* no.

Amazing! The whole time they were kids, they never tired. Or at least admitted it. And kids won't admit it. The reason they won't admit it is because if they do, you may make them take a nap. And kids hate naps. Fact is, aside from taking a bath, nothing can be worse for a kid than taking a nap.

Parents, on the other hand, would kill for a nap. It's funny how it works. Kids never get tired but parents are exhausted.

Our youngest recently played the role of a parent when he told his mother (who was having a very bad day) that perhaps she needed to go to her room and take a nap. Her look of uncontainable glee at the mere suggestion was not what he expected. "Oh yes," she said, "pleeeeese send me to my room!"

I remember years ago putting our oldest daughter down for a nap. I read her a story and then stayed quiet and still until she fell asleep. But she never did. She was smart enough to wait until I fell asleep (which didn't take long) so she could get back to the business of playing. So much for naptime.

I used to make fun of my father for turning on the television, cranking his recliner into third gear and falling asleep in front of a blaring ballgame. I never understood why older people would do that. I do now. You will never believe this but...many a night my wife wakes me up to go to bed.

Raising kids is exhausting and endless work. But it's worth it. Fact is, it is one of the few pursuits in life in which the payoff is greater than the investment. Training our offspring, building into their lives solid character, and inspiring them to reach their goals will leave behind a legacy that benefits generations to come. That's what I call an investment—and it's the best one you will ever make.

But sometimes it's hard to see. Especially when you're tired and too pooped to parent. But hang in there. And when the tables turn and your kid sends you to your room, *seize the moment*! One piece of advice: leave the door cracked and an eye open because...parents are never off duty.

People and Preachers

I'm a preacher. There, I said it. I feel somewhat like the folks down at A.A. who understand the need for full confession. Fact is, sometimes it's not easy admitting you are one (a preacher, that is) and for good reason. People get really weird around preachers. I've had extra seats open up on airplanes just because I pull out a Bible and start working. "You a preacher?" asks a seatmate. "Why, yes I am," comes the reply. "You know," says the stranger, carefully negotiating his carry-on in one hand and his beer in the other, "uh, I think there might be some empty seats back yonder some place—and I'm sure you need a little extra room..." Works every time.

It's like the little boy who didn't know that the preacher had dropped by for a visit to his home. He rushed in and held up a dead rat by the tail. "Look Mom!" he exclaimed.

"Look at this rat Tommy and I caught. We trapped it and then we hit it with baseball bats, we smashed its brains out, and spit on it and stomped it and..."—and then seeing the visitor in the corner, he lowered his head, removed his hat, and proclaimed solemnly, "and then...and then the Lord called him home."

See what I mean?

People also lie to you. Like the fellow a few years ago who bragged that my Sunday sermon was the finest he had ever heard. I wanted to say, "That's funny, because you slept through the whole thing!" I didn't say that because preachers are supposed to be experts at diplomacy.

I have a friend who didn't do too well as a preacher. He was gifted for sure—but it was a gift for usually saying the wrong thing. Like the time at the hospital when he walked into a room and tried to comfort a church member going into surgery, "Wow," he said. "You look terrible. I hope you don't die or something..." He must have missed the diplomacy part.

There are job hazards with this profession. Like making sure you use the right words. I heard of a guy who kept preaching about how fun it was going to be in heaven with all that "immorality." Funny how close immo***ral***ity and immor***tal***ity can sound.

Then there was the country fellow who told me why he never had to take any notes when listening to my sermons. "The good Lord has blessed me with a pornographic memory..."

People are funny. Especially around preachers.

Peace Lodge

I write these words from a rocking chair on the front porch of Peace Lodge. *Peace Lodge* isn't the official name of this tranquil mountain hideaway; it's my name. It is my own designation given to one of the calmest, quietest and most reflective places I have ever been. There may be locations more majestic but there is none more soothing to the soul or inspiring to the heart than *Peace Lodge.*

Sometimes it helps to get away. Sometimes it's necessary to leave the rat race to the rats and take a cleansing breath of nature's freshness. Busyness, deadlines and the pressures of daily commitments seem to fade in the serene mountain air. Television, terrorists, and international turmoil appear especially distant from a wooden rocking chair on a mountain front porch. Yes, sometimes we need to push the pause button on life and step back occasionally from the proliferation of troubles—both national and international—and renew our souls.

This place is a small, unadvertised Bed and Breakfast nestled away in the mountains of Virginia. Barely. It's just a stone's throw to Kentucky and an hour north of Tennessee's Tri-Cities. If you crave shopping, entertainment, and crowds, go to places like Pigeon Forge. If your soul seeks solitude, follow the path less taken to Peace Lodge.

A River Runs Through It is more than Hollywood here; it's real. So are the waterfalls. Beyond the pasture and across the river rise the mountains that are alive with the colorful touches of the Master's hand. October oranges, reds, and bright golds are set against a sky of deepened blue. There is a feel of autumn in the breeze. Deer and wild turkey are abundant. And so are bass in the pond.

I spoke three times this morning and will address an audience again tonight in a nearby town. That's work. It may be a labor of love but it is still taxing and tiring. But mixed between the business of public speaking is the need to bring order to my private world. Times like this help. Places like this help.

Something tells me that I will find my way back to this serene and simple place. So will others. It's not the kind of place easily kept a secret for very long. But even if I am unable to return, I can always close my eyes, take a minute mental journey, and soothe my mind with the memories of this quiet hideaway.

Goodbye stress. Hello, *Peace Lodge.*

Women Are From Venus; Men Are From?

We men are odd creatures. (That got a hearty "A-men!" from every woman in town!) It's true. Masculinity is as impossible to articulate as it is to understand. For example, the hunter instinct in the male species will cause him to drive twenty miles in the wrong direction before admitting he hasn't a clue where he is (if he indeed ever admits it at all). A female, on the other hand, feels a natural urge to stop at the nearest gas station and ask for directions (provided they have clean restrooms). My wife and I compromise: I drive ten miles and then ask.

A man will get upset because his wife spends a few dollars too much on groceries (which he eats!) or buys a new outfit at the mall—only to turn around and buy a new...*boat?* 'Course if he bought it on sale and saved thousands, it's okay.

Women just don't understand us. Maybe it's because every man was once a little boy—a little boy with big dreams:

dreams of being the hero, beating the bad guy and saving the girl. Oh yes, and hitting the home run in the bottom of the ninth to win the World Series.

Men were created with a rugged itch for adventure. A woman often marries a man because she is intrigued and captivated by his wilder side, only to spend the rest of her life trying to domesticate him. But (and here is the kicker!) if she wins, she loses. She loses the real man she married. "How can I get my husband to have more passion?" she asks. Simple. Invite him to be the man he was made to be. (Translated: move the Thomas Kinkade picture to the bedroom and put his ten-pointer back over the fireplace.)

It's simple psychology. For example, when a man sports hair on the chin, it's a psychological signal that says *I'm a little wild.* Then again, when you see him with his baseball caps turned backwards it means: *I'm still a little boy.*

It's why little boys love to wrestle, climb trees, and play with toy guns. It's the challenge of adventure and it's built in. My youngest son is eight and loves nothing better than to take on his dad in a little game of one-on-one tackle football. It's nothing short of the ageless ritual of the young buck challenging the old bull. My oldest son is twenty-two. When he wants to take on his dad in a game of tackle, I find every convenient reason (excuse?) not to engage. I have this phobia about orthopedic surgery.

A little advice to all you moms and wives: be patient with us. We're men. We're strong and stubborn; brave of heart and wild at heart; adventuresome and a little aggressive. We're men. Enough said.

Lone Star and Three Stars

The sun is ris'
The sun is set,
And we ain't out
Of Texas yet.

I spend a lot of time in Texas. Texans are known for their Lone Star pride and statewide (and it is a very wide state!) braggadocio—after all, everything is bigger in Texas! From bluebonnets to beef brisket, from longhorns to ten-gallon hats, Texans have a lot for which to be proud. I love Texas and I love Texans because the Lone Star State combines two things for which I have a fondness—the south and the west.

When Russ Bowman, my Beaumont friend, married an Alabama girl, the prospect of repeating those sacred vows away from the holy ground of Texas soil bothered him to the point that he scooped up his beloved Texas dirt and took it with him. To this day he proudly claims that while he may not have been married "in" Texas, he was married "on" Texas. Some things are that important.

Several years ago, I took my oldest son to watch a baseball series in Arlington between the Texas Rangers and the Baltimore Orioles. It was there that he met (in his opinion) the greatest Texan of all time. No, it wasn't George Bush, the owner of the ball club and eventual President of the United States—it was none other than Mr. Advil himself: Nolan Ryan. Sorry, Mr. President.

Did you know that Texas has a distinct Tennessee flavor when it comes to history? Thirty Tennessee volunteers lost their life at the Alamo while fighting bravely for Texas independence—including the coonskin, sharpshootin', fiddle playin', yarn spinnin' Davy Crockett. And Sam Houston, for which the nation's fourth largest city was eventually named, was a Tennessee congressman and governor before he led his men to victory over the despised Mexican general Santa Anna. Even today, there are a lot of transplanted Tennesseans in Texas.

Maybe that's why folks in the Lone Star State mention Tennessee with a tone of fondness. If I have heard it once, I have heard it a hundred times–from Amarillo to Austin, from Houston to Ft. Worth–"Oh, you're from Tennessee? We just love it there!"

Texans fly the flag of the old Lone Star with a pride and patriotic zeal that is as big as the state. And well they should. Tennesseans, likewise, proudly parade their three stars–three stars that represent the uniqueness of a simple tri-fold land that cools its feet in the mighty Mississippi and lays its head in the serene pillows of the great Smoky Mountains. And somewhere in between she finds solace in the breezes of the easy flowing Cumberland and the rolling green hills of her mid-land.

Tennessee has been described in a lot of ways but the best definition of all is this: *home*. There is something special about her slower pace and gentle kindness, her peaceful seasons and southern charm that call us back home. Maybe my Murfreesboro friend, Jim Deason, said it best when he proclaimed, "I may not have been born here, but I got here as fast as I could."

Lone Star or Three Stars. *Texas* or *Tennessee*. Either way, I like the way that sounds.

I Still Believe

You better watch out, You better not cry,
You better not pout, I'm telling you why...
Santa Claus is coming to town.

I don't remember exactly when I found out–you know, the *real* story about Santa Claus and how everything worked. I was probably in the third grade when the talk made the rounds on the playground and I first heard those awful and never-to-be-forgotten words–"There is no such thing as Santa Claus."

No. It can't be. It just can't be. Fact is, I had seen him at the shopping center and in the Christmas parade. It wasn't just anyone dressed in red, it was *him*! And I had seen him on television. He may have been in black and white in those days, but my imagination painted him bright red. No. It was *him*!

For the longest time I didn't say anything. I was afraid to. *What if*...they were wrong? *What if*...they were right? *What if*...I said I didn't believe and then on Christmas morning... No. They were wrong. They had to be wrong. There were even presents under the tree that said: "From Santa." Besides, the milk and cookies were always gone the next morning. Always. And next to the empty plate would be a note saying, "Thanks for the cookies. I gave one to Rudolph. Mr. C." I didn't need any more proof than that. I still believed.

He came to my grandparent's house one night. We had gone there that year for Christmas and about bedtime there was a knock at the door. My grandfather spoke in my direction, "Better get that, Hot Shot." I opened the door and began to back away slowly with mouth open and eyes big and getting bigger. It was *him*! He wasn't like the play Santa on the pretend sleigh in my grandpa's front yard, he was *real*. He came inside, took me in his arms and told me that he knew I had been a very good boy. And then, with a jolly chorus of "Ho, Ho, Ho," he reached into his bag and gave me a gift. I will never forget that night. And when he left I watched through the window as he drove out of sight—not in a sleigh with eight tiny reindeer but in a '61 Buick that looked a lot like brother Bill Smith's Buick from church.

Years later, I would do the same thing. Renting a Santa suit and making the rounds to children from church, I will never forget their little faces and bright smiles. I remember going to the home of some foster kids. Those kids hugged me so tight and so long that I thought they would never let go. I wouldn't sell those memories for a million dollars. No way.

Sadly, some parents do a disservice to their children by robbing them of the innocent imagination of childhood. Imagination is a precious gift that God gives to children. It is this God-given innocence and sense of wonder that helps to cushion their introduction into a world that will all too quickly become harsh and complicated.

Some parents think that their children will grow up hating them or somehow distrusting them if they allow them to believe the Santa story. Funny thing, I've never met any of those kids. In fact, I'm thankful my parents played the childhood game and allowed me to live in my own little world of innocent adventure and imagination. And we have done the same for our children. Was it a good thing? Ask them.

Children grow up too fast these days. For whatever reason, we're afraid to allow them to be exactly who they are—

children. We think we have to logically explain everything to them on an adult level—from the facts of life to the fact that the dinosaur in the purple suit is really a man in a costume whose name isn't "Barney." Good grief. Can't kids be "kids" anymore?

Imagination is the fuel that rockets a child through his world. It's why children love Disney World and cartoons and fictitious fairy-tale stories. It's why they sleep with stuffed animals and play with imaginary friends. And it's why it is nothing but innocent make-believe to allow them to believe in Santa Claus.

The day will come when he will hear the talk on the playground and begin to question. In fact, he will begin to question long before he ever comes and asks you. But when that day comes, take him in your arms, explain how it really works and gradually bring him out of his precious childhood. But not too fast. By the way, our two still left at home know the "scoop" about Mr. C., but...we still put out the milk and cookies every Christmas Eve. And when the last child is grown and gone, we'll continue to put out the milk and cookies. Because... I still believe.

Besides, Santa may need something to munch on while driving home in his Buick.

Togwotee

Togwotee. I'll get to that in a moment.

Like so many towns that dot the American landscape, ours has developed a greenway. You can walk, jog, bike, or roller blade for several miles on a wide paved path, accented by long wooden bridges that span meandering creeks. It is a mind-soothing walk to remember any time of the year, but especially when spring blossoms or fall colors accent the path. If you're lucky, you may even see deer or raccoons foraging for food. This environmentally-friendly path through the woods, however, is costly—and I'm talking more than tax dollars. I'm talking about a nine-year-old kid on a bike next to mine who thinks that it is mandatory to cool off with one of those flavorful slushy drinks after an afternoon ride. I don't know who thought of putting the greenway parking lot next to our local Sonic Drive-In—but it makes for good math. Now you can *add* back all the calories you just *subtracted*. Then again, it ranks up there with other conscience-soothing American diet plans—like eating a candy bar while consuming a diet cola. I guess it all balances out.

A word of appreciation is in order for every small town Police and Fire Department. These folks do a great job serving and protecting America's communities without the fanfare of larger departments and sometimes with little thanks. They do more than lead our parades and endear themselves to wide-eyed children on field trips to the local firehouse or police station. These folks sacrifice their time (and sometimes their lives) and respond 24/7 to our calls for help. I am proud to have a son who is a policeman. I am proud to have a son-in-law who is a fireman. To them and to all who proudly serve us—consider this a community-wide, nationwide: "Thank you."

A good friend of mine is currently flying Blackhawk missions in Afghanistan. I read the other day that there is a 9½ hour time difference between Nashville, Tennessee and Afghanistan. Okay, nine hours I can understand. Ten hours I can understand. But the ½? What's that? (Listen, I have enough trouble meeting my eastern time Louisville, Kentucky parents for dinner near Mammoth Cave and working out the—"my time" versus "your time" scenario). But here's my question: Do Afghans "spring forward" in April like we do? And if they "spring," do they spring ½ hour? The world is a very funny place.

Remember the anthrax scare a few years ago? Like a lot of things, there was more misunderstanding than truth. Like the fellow who declared that the whole problem could be solved if people would just stay off trains. Trains??? It's "anthrax"—not *Amtrak*!

There are some great people in every small town—great because they don't know they are. Folks like Ron and Doris Williams who own and operate our hometown printing shop. It's a small business but a staple (pun intended!) of our community. In addition to their involvement here, the Williams's just returned from two months in Africa where they helped people in a less advantaged corner of the world get their own printing shop up and running. And just as their culture cannot fathom ours, the opposite is also true. "I cried when I got there," said Doris, "and I cried when I left." Life, it's really all about the people—no matter where they live.

Togwotee. It's an Indian name meaning, "that from here, you can go anywhere." Maybe that's one of the great things about my small town—and yours. You can start here and travel to distant lands. Then again, it begs the question of...who would ever want to leave? Togwotee.

Morning Glory

I couldn't sleep this morning. I don't know why exactly but after tossing and turning for half an hour, I decided that there must be something more productive to do with one's time and so...I left the house about 5:30 and went for a walk.

It was an absolutely beautiful middle Tennessee morning. The fog lay heavy along the ground, obscuring all but the very tops of the trees and barns. Through the morning mist and high above, the nearly full moon glowed with a brilliant white as it reflected the sunlight that was yet to arrive below. There is something very special about being alive in the early morning when everything is fresh and new. I walked on.

Off in the distance you could hear the sounds of trucks and traffic from one of the nation's busiest interstates—a testimony to the value of man's productivity and hard work. Below my feet, a field mouse scampered near the edge of the path—a testimony that all things big and small engage in activity ordered by their Maker. I walked on.

About a mile later and through the distant fog I could barely make out the silhouette of a man. We were walking in opposite directions, he going west and I going east, both of us sharing a certain commonness–both of us were created in the image of God and both of us were enjoying the first light of His new day. "Good morning," I said to the stranger with a wave. "Beautiful morning for walking," said he. I smiled and proclaimed, "Indeed it is." I walked on.

As the road followed the crooked path of a meandering stream, I rounded a bend and saw a house that showed not the slightest sign of life. I imagined the inhabitants enjoying a few final moments of slumber before awakening to the sunny dawn. And I saw their dog–stretched lazily across the front step, oblivious to a stranger's approach. Since I was at the end of my route and needing to turn back anyway (and since I remembered an old saying about "letting sleeping dogs lie"), I quietly turned and retraced my steps toward home. I walked on.

Finally, through the misty morning, there it was. It isn't much by the world's standard but it is by my standards. It's not the house or the land that makes it special; it's the people inside. Thus, as I took the final steps of a joyful walk, I thanked God for His grace and goodness and...for His simple gift of morning glory. I shook my head at the wonder of it all. And walked on.